MW00791140

In Search of the Most Amazing Thing

Children, Education, and Computers

Tom Snyder *&* Jane Palmer

ADDISON-WESLEY PUBLISHING COMPANY, INC.

Reading, Massachusetts   Menlo Park, California   New York
Don Mills, Ontario   Wokingham, England Amsterdam Bonn
Sidney Singapore Tokyo Madrid San Juan Paris
Seoul Milan Mexico City Taipei

To Bill, who said it could be done

Library of Congress Cataloging-in-Publication Data

Snyder, Tom.
  In search of the most amazing thing.

  Bibliography: p.
  Includes index.
  1. Computer-assisted instruction. 2. Computers and children. I.
Palmer, Jane. II. Title.
LB1028.5.S63 1986   371.3'9445   86-1142
ISBN 0-201-16437-X

Cover design by Steve Snider
Text design by Anna Post, Cambridge, MA
Text set in 10 pt. Baskerville by DEKR Corp., Woburn, MA
3 4 5 6 7 8 9 10 - DO - 9594939291
Third printing, November 1991

CONTENTS

ACKNOWLEDGMENTS *v*

1 What Is Going On Here? *1*

2 Great Expectations *7*

3 Real Life *23*

4 In Search of the Most Amazing Thing *51*

5 The Indefatigable Drillmaster *75*

6 Mind Tools *91*

7 It's How You Play the Game *105*

BIBLIOGRAPHY *144*

INDEX *151*

ACKNOWLEDGMENTS

Many thanks are due to many people. Among them are Henry Olds, David Dockterman, Judah Schwartz, Joseph Weizenbaum, David Miller, Rick Abrams, David Perkins, David Seuss, Martha O'Neill, Peter Kelman, Jock McClees, Nancy Roberts, David Bouchard, Stanley Kugell, John Mulcahey, Leslie Greenfield, Joyce Fitzgerald, Susan Fahlund, Harry White, Caroline Palmer, Al Palmer, and William Bellows.

1.

What Is Going On Here?

If this book didn't exist by now it would have to be invented. Why? Because we have a problem. In the past few years, the nation's schools have opened their doors to the computer in the hopes that it would help them prepare millions of children for the "information age." This was done with the avid support of the hardware and software industries which, in the interests of exploiting a new and lucrative market, have spared no effort in making their case convincing. Their incentives are such that only a massive revolution can make their investment cost effective. The problem is that schools have responded too hastily, too eagerly, and at too great a cost to justify what they're getting. Teachers watching billions of dollars worth of technology stream in are so excited by its potential that they fail to notice how meager are its real achievements.

Ironically, education is not a profession this society rewards with much money or recognition. On the contrary, it tends to be held in faint contempt, and its institutions and practitioners are the first to be blamed for an endless list of problems ranging from widespread illiteracy to the latest bugbear, *computer illiter-*

1

acy. In 1983, the National Commission on Excellence in Education issued its ringing indictment in *A Nation at Risk: The Imperative for Educational Reform*:

> The educational foundations of our society are presently being eroded by a rising tide of mediocrity that threatens our very future as a nation and a people.

Before and since, "the crisis in education" is the topic of an article every other week in every other popular news magazine. Under the circumstances, a profession-wide sense of insecurity is inevitable, as is a certain susceptibility to claims that a solution is just around the corner.

The computer, in a sense bordering on conflict of interest, has become both the problem and the solution. An understanding *of the machine* is near the top of our list of things kids need to have to be educated. This machine has simultaneously been shown to be effective in helping children learn everything from shape recognition to advanced calculus, and in helping them think creatively, with a better grasp of how things work, including computers. It has also been put forward as an inherently motivating, inexhaustible replacement for teachers themselves. Without much effort, one can find claims for the computer as a solution to just about anything. It's better than snake oil! And a lot more expensive.

There is no question but that the computer is an important factor in our lives today and even more so in our children's lives, which stretch further into the future. It therefore seems reasonable that an effort be made to prepare children for life with computers, although what kind of effort is not entirely clear. It seems reasonable as well to take advantage of the computer when and how it can be useful in instruction.

But we must not lose sight of our paramount objective, which is, of course, ensuring our children's educational well-being. Isn't this what we're after when we send our kids to school? Isn't this what we fault the schools for failing at? Of course. And this too is the source of our interest in bringing computers into the schools. But the technology itself is so compelling that we've shifted our focus, without really noticing, from the kids to the computer. We're more interested in so-called computer literacy than the real thing, *literacy*, and more keen to put our children in front of a machine than a book or a map or even other kids. It is time (overdue!) to figure out what is going on here. What are our educational priorities? What can the computer do to support them? What can it not do? We need to find out.

This book is both a reminder and a guide. It was conceived in the spring of 1984, when schools and software companies were still riding high on hopes for educational computing and "shakeout" was mentioned only in whispers, like someone else's impending divorce. In the interim, the industry, which had been made to flourish by huge infusions of venture capital, slowed down to a crawl as the money flow was slowed by investors no longer willing to subsidize companies that made no market sense. Technological innovation in the schools all but stalled. These developments, however, have not mitigated the sense of urgency that drives this book. It is as important now as it was in 1984 to keep our use of the technology in proportion to our true educational needs.

The facts and fictions of educational computing are the subject of the first half of this book.

FACT: *We do not know how to use the new technology to support education on a mass scale.* We *act* as if we did. We commit ourselves to the technology as if certain of where it's taking us or at least that any minute now the proper course will become clear. A few experiments have shown us wonderful ways a few children can learn a few things, but most of what is being done these days is disappointing. Without more experience, we should hesitate to so heavily mortgage our children's future. We might do well to set as a goal nothing more (or less) than a long stretch of loose, inexpensive experimentation with educational computing. We could call it a "fool-around period."

FACT: *Computers cannot teach.* Impressive as they are, computers can do almost nothing directly either to inspire or facilitate learning. This is what teachers do, and with support they can do it very, very well. Yet it is as a teaching machine that the computer is most often used in schools, with software known as CAI, or computer-aided instruction. Other approaches might be more fruitful, especially those which recognize the indispensible human component in teaching and learning. The teacher *must* be included.

With the help of good teachers, educational software can transform the machine from a box to a ballgame to something instructive. The second half of this book is about software — what it is, how it works, what if anything it has to offer our children and their teachers. Chapters 5, 6, and 7 follow a three-part taxonomy introduced in Chapter 3. In this system, devised by Henry F. Olds, Jr., senior editor of *Classroom Computer Learning*, the computer is classified as an instructional medium, a tool, and a modeling device. In the first category, using CAI software, the computer functions as an automated teacher of facts and procedures. As a tool, it is available like any other tool to do the user's bidding. One only needs to learn how to handle it, through programming or any of the ready-made, general-purpose programs such as word processing or numerical analysis. As a modeling device, the computer is used, with software games and simulations, not so much to teach as to create environments supportive of teaching.

The authors must admit to a certain bias in favor of this last approach. Games and simulations represent at once the most unassuming and least appreciated type of educational software. They actively support an interaction *between people* that is often ignored by other software, and it is this social content which the authors find appealing. It is also astonishingly powerful.

Tom's views derive from several years' experience as a school teacher and educational software designer, occupations which he chose in part because of his experiences as a "bad" student. "I was very active in projects," he explains, "but I couldn't figure out how to do well in school. I always wanted to know why things were important, and no one would tell me. They just said '*Do it*'." As a teacher at Shady Hill School in Cambridge, Massachusetts, Tom had his first chance to offset this arbitrariness by making sure his students knew what they were learning and why. He used the computer to simulate environments which amplified his opportunities to teach and let all the kids join in as active learners. The success of these first programs, and the lack of others like them, prompted Tom to take them to market. His company, Tom Snyder Productions, has since developed a number of highly acclaimed educational games and simulations, as well as programs for teachers.

Unlike Tom, Jane was a "good" student, an achievement she attributes largely to responding on cue. Jane's vantage point is farther from the scene, as she is not a teacher or software designer, but a writer, and this was a story to tell. It is also closer, for she was the one with the tape recorder, who put pencil to paper (and fingers to keys) to bring this book from the impassioned front line to the printed page.

And none too soon. Our schools are still in unrelieved jeopardy of committing themselves prematurely to a course that fails both to benefit from the technology and to take care of our children's education.

There are no answers here, no step-by-step instructions in how to buy educational software. Readers seeking such instruction will need to look elsewhere, in any of the numerous magazines and booklets which do not hesitate to formalize the rules. Checklists, guidelines, and standards abound in those publications. Each set includes the implication that one need only choose *which* set to follow in order to proceed with confident peace of mind. This book includes no formal software standards, for one of its messages is to the contrary, that arbitrary rules are necessarily invalid. The success of a piece of software, like all additives to the learning process, is utterly dependent on the way it is handled and in what context. Guidelines may help us make informed choices, but they do nothing to relieve each one of us of the *obligation* to evaluate the stuff for ourselves and to apply it in a fashion appropriate to the situation. Guidelines also tend to pull our attention rather too much in the direction of the technology, as if all we had to do was look hard enough to find the answer. It's not there. Not yet, anyway; maybe never; it is much too early to tell. In the meantime, we'd be wise to take a look at our expectations for educational technology, for they have almost as much to do with where we're going as the technology itself.

2.

Great Expectations

The computer revolution is upon us, according to the wisdom. We're knee-deep in the sparkling eighties, about to be wired into a world-wide communications grid providing each of us access, via computers, to information banks, events calendars, weather reports, electronic news and mail, reproduction of documents, banking, shopping, credit cards — and education. The spectrum of current fantasies runs from life without school, where education is a do-it-yourself enterprise, to school as a sort of electronic beehive with every student buzzing at his or her own wildly capable workstation. The common dream-theme is access to data in quantities heretofore unimaginable, awesome computing capability, and software for most subjects under the sun.

There are those in favor and those against. Some are thrilled to be surging toward a Toffleresque brave new world. Others recoil as if at something morally offensive. In the middle is the largest group — parents and teachers — who wonder what will happen next and what they should do about it.

The present wave of high hopes arose in the late 1970s, when the commercial availability of microcomputers coincided with one of those periodic attacks on teachers, who were said not to be doing their job. Students' test scores were plummeting and schools were getting panned. Something had to be done about the mess we were in and it seemed, in the glowing light of the new technology, that the thing to do was computerize education. A *Time* survey in December 1982, found that 57 percent of Americans thought personal computers would enable their children "to read and do math better." Intense propaganda from hardware and software manufacturers lent support to this belief. In January 1983, Control Data's vice president for education strategy said, "If you want to improve youngsters one grade level in reading, our PLATO program with teacher supervision can do it up to four times faster and for 40 percent less expense than teachers alone." Computers would replace human teachers, according to other, incautious futurists. We would push the teacher-student ratio to 1:50 or higher. Computers would either redeem our schools or eliminate the need for them altogether. These visions, although they have lost some of their luster, still glimmer from afar.

David Perkins is Director of Project Zero, a basic research program at the Harvard Graduate School of Education investigating cognitive-symbolic capacities and their implications. At a 1983 symposium on video games and human development, he described the hope of "educational heaven" gleaming in many an eye.

> Educational heaven is there in your own living room perhaps a decade away. You have a couple of mini-computers. You own a sizable collection of educational software, software written in various game formats. The software covers entire subject areas — algebra, history, spelling, English composition, and so on — with rigor and flair.... No longer do you need to badger your offspring to study. This new style of education has all the lure of today's video games. Now students study out of enthusiasm rather than coercion.

David Seuss, president of the educational software company, Spinnaker Software, envisions a better world where control of education is in the hands of parents and children. Where kids who can read and use a computer can take care of their own learning. Where parents choose from among a couple of dozen competing curriculum software packages (their choice between drill-and-practice, tutorials, learning games, simulations), spending through a voucher or tax credit system the money that had formerly been earmarked for schools. "Parents are intuitive," says Seuss, "so they'd be good at providing education." Educator John Holt asserts that even the nicest, most concerned of teachers cannot know as much about teaching a child as can a good parent.

Seymour Papert has conceived some of the loveliest, most intriguing visions. Author of *Mindstorms: Children, Computers, and Powerful Ideas*, lead inventor of LOGO, and MIT professor of mathematics and education, he urges that computers be as available as pencils "for scribbling as well as for writing, doodling as well as drawing, for illicit notes as well as for official classroom assignments." He seeks to reverse the standard pattern wherein, as he puts it, the computer programs the child. He would rather have the child program the computer. His hypothetical Mathland is a place where learning mathematics would be as natural as learning French in France. Children would use computers designed so that the process of learning to communicate with them is a natural one; math would be a living language. And learning to communicate with a "math-speaking" computer would in turn facilitate other learning. Children in Mathland would be the "builders of their own intellectual structures," drawing from materials they find about them, including computers, which could make concepts simple and concrete.

Under one of Papert's wings, the Boston Public Schools launched a five-year project in March 1985 to turn Hennigan Elementary School into the "technology school of the future." Hennigan, chosen among the city's eighty elementary schools, has been loaded up with computers and software, the teachers trained at MIT summer workshops, and the classrooms graced with educational technologists. At Hennigan, according to Papert, the computers will be used "in art, in math, in writing" to make education "more open, more child-centered, more successful." Cost is something over $1 million, courtesy of IBM.

The results from Papert's other experiments are stirring, albeit sketchy. There is Marlon, who once saw someone shot, who is poor, angry, behind in a school that looks like a nineteenth-century prison but which is the site of an experiment involving one computer for every four children and a twice monthly visit from Dr. Papert. The New York City school system had spent $18,000 in trying, unsuccessfully, to teach Marlon to read, but now the boy is reading. Reading! Because he wants to find out how to use the computer, because reading at last means something to him. Marlon is in touch for the first time in his life with what Papert calls "a sense of intellectual power." Papert is too modest to suggest that LOGO is the sole agent here, or the only hope in years to come. He offers his LOGO environments as models, or prototypes, for educationally powerful computational environments that might provide alternatives to traditional modes of teaching. They are collectively his candle against the darkness.

Another great purveyor of such visions is Sherry Turkle, author of *The Second Self: Computers and the Human Spirit*. She has given us perhaps the most far-reaching evidence of how children can learn with computers. How, in the unfettered hands of children with widely diverse styles and proclivities, the computer can become an object (or is it a subject?) of glorious, seemingly near-human complexity. Turkle makes clear that this "object-to-think-with" need not be the exclusive province of "hard," math-oriented types, but can be as well a combination muse and magic wand for the "soft" types, the dreamers and artists and those who sat in the corner until the computer came along.

There is Kevin, a fourth grader enchanted with the prospect of creating on the screen a rocket's fiery red flare. Unlike his wizard classmate Jeff, Kevin works with the computer in a loose, intuitive fashion, not in an effort to impose his will on the screen but to create exciting visual effects. There is Ronnie, a third grader who comes to school dancing, a radio clamped to his head, who is bright but doing badly in school. In the course of devising a program to make thirty-two little colored balls dance "perfectly" (by which he means that "the balls should go right to the edge"), Ronnie learns some key algebraic concepts he undoubtedly would never have come to along the standard route. And there is Deborah, who encountered the computer when she was an overweight, insecure, temperamental, unhappy eleven-year-old. She started with one arbitrary rule — she could command the LOGO turtle to make only right turns of 30 degrees — and from there developed a tiny world within the computer. Deborah was successful in this tight little world and could apply some of its lessons about rules and control to her temper, her eating, her numerous other problems. "You program yourself how to be," she said.

Turkle, Papert, and the other visionaries are doubtless on to something important. They have shown through their experiments and observations that the computer can indeed have a powerful, positive influence on education. They have pushed the range of real possibilities far wider than had previously been considered, and thereby set up a challenge both to proponents and opponents of educational computing. Their work answers many questions; it raises more.

You Can't Get There from Here

The positive results of such experiments are genuine in each case. The problem is that the specific does not necessarily generalize. What we have here are the fruits of experimental environments that are, in computerphile terms, ideal. Whether they're ideal in other terms is an open question, but in any event, such creative uses are neither typical of educational computing in the schools today nor are they likely to be in the future. What works for each child cannot be provided to that child indefinitely, nor can it be offered to all. Deborah no longer has ready access to a computer because the experiment at her school is over. The kids in Marlon's apartment building and the ones he plays with on the street do not partake of the joys of computing — never have, probably never will. It would take an effort of considerably greater proportions to make educational heaven a reality for the millions of Marlons, Deborahs, Kevins, and Ronnies we as a nation are committed and required, by law, to educate. In the meantime, experiments aside, mainstream experience with computers in education is not quite what we had hoped. It is disappointing. Mediocre. Hardly the stuff of dreams.

The champions tell us not to worry, because all revolutions are messy, and all new media are underutilized or utilized inappropriately in their first few years on the scene. "Almost everything being done with computers in the schools is bad," says Papert, dismissing as a sort of coltish awkwardness the trivial and superficial applications.

> It took years before designers of automobiles accepted the idea that they were cars, not "horseless carriages," and the precursors of modern motion pictures were plays acted as if before a live audience but actually in front of a camera. A whole generation was needed for the new art of motion pictures to emerge as something quite different from a linear mix of theater plus photography. Most of what has been done up to now under the name of "educational technology" or "computers in education" is still at the stage of the linear mix of old instructional methods with new technologies.

Papert's attitude is one of patient impatience, as if all we had to do was get beyond the tiresome linear mixes to find the good stuff. It is shared to varying degrees by the whole crowd of futurists and behind them, doggedly, nearly everyone else. We simultaneously comfort and prod ourselves with the thought that the technology is only as good as we make it. ("Otherwise," as Edward R. Murrow said about television, "it is merely lights and wires in a box.") We're convinced at an almost subliminal level that our problems are transitional, and that all we need to do, more or less, is something useful with educational computing.

Yes, but there is more to it than that. Sure, this is a revolution — one of the first in history to be conducted with this degree of self-consciousness — but let's take it as slowly as we possibly can. The technology is running away with us like a pack of wild horses, and we should do what we can to hold in the reins. We should appreciate, not disparage, the sluggishness with which the culture embraces (or refrains from embracing) computer technology. And we should recognize that it isn't easy to do "something useful," for what is useful must emerge from a careful union of what is and what is needed.

Furthermore, there are dangers in our great expectations and in our headlong rush to fulfill them. Despite preliminary cynicism and disappointment, we are still under the influence of a hope more ephemeral than realistic. In fact, the computer has done little that is educationally significant. What it has done is capture our imagination, and prompt us to finance possibly the biggest *unfocused* research effort in the world at a cost, for hardware and software alone, projected to exceed $8 billion in 1987. So compelling are the continuing fantasies that they overshadow debate about the merits of educational computing relative to other priorities. They persuade us *not* to ask some important questions — not the hows, but the whys and whats, as in *What are we really trying to accomplish?* and, *Why should the schools be the one major group to pay the bill?* The error is dynamic. It is throwing us, like a clay pot gone awry, farther and farther off-center.

Where Angels Fear to Tread

Perhaps the greatest danger of disproportionate expectations, as noted by Joseph Weizenbaum, MIT professor of computer science, is in inducing us to take huge risks with an entire generation of children. While we're no longer so naive as to think of computers as the silicon embodiment of the Second Coming, we have, following our first brush with disappointment, simply flattened and diluted our expectations, made them more pedestrian. While state and federal money has stopped gushing into the schools, and the computer industry has fallen on hard times, we nevertheless hold tight to the core fantasy of some version of computer-based heaven. We remain convinced that any day now (has it already come?) computers will so alter the way we live and work that life as we know it is already an antique. On the strength of this conviction, parents are still buying educational software at an annual rate expected to reach three-quarters of a billion dollars by 1987. Schools will make up the other quarter billion.

Some of us may be relieved by the market downturn. We may breathe great sighs of relief that computers are no longer a craze but a commonplace. But the very commonness of the technology has become a spur to further educational application. The use of computers in every other nook and cranny, from automated banking to missle guidance to "intelligent" sewing machines, has been allowed to carry with it the powerful suggestion that computers are therefore a necessary ingredient in our children's education. We jump from an observation of the pervasiveness of the technology to the conclusion that we should use it to provide better, faster, more effective education. As in the more hot-headed seventies, this argument is reinforced by the unsettling feeling that schools — not just teachers but the entire institution — are not doing their job. It is assumed that educators must teach with computers and about them. Why? Because they're there. Because it's hip, because it's good for us (good for the mind, for the sense of mastery). And because if we don't, we and our children will be left in the dust. "The speed of development in computer technology," warned a report by the New York State Department of Education Commission in 1981, "threaten[s] to divide people into 'technocrats' and 'technopeasants,' those who can keep up with change (and, thus, to a certain extent, control it) and those who cannot. Education has an obvious mission to close the gap."

It is facile to argue that these problems would take care of themselves if we gave to all children the computer opportunities enjoyed by Marlon and Deborah. This is not enough; paradoxically, it may already be too much. The hysteria with which we regard the coming of the information age, with which we press computers onto the schools, may itself be to blame for the widening gaps and the otherwise disappointing applications. We create myth as much as reality when we equate computer skills with success and with-it-ness. It does not have to be so.

The reality of educational computing in the trenches — not at Hennigan Elementary or in Mathland, but in Hometown, USA — is rather drab and equivocal at the moment. Just how drab will be explored in the following chapter. Yet as great as the disappointment, it hasn't come close to overwhelming the power of the great expectations. The movement remains potentially so expensive and so risky that it is incumbent upon everyone involved in making decisions about education to keep debate at the fore. Attention is currently fixed upon the impact of computers on society, on industry and education, without much thought to the reverse. We are allowing computers to rearrange our priorities simply by default. The dream of school-based educational heaven has already been institutionalized and as such is no longer a dream, no longer under constant scrutiny. The fantasy is all the more dangerous for being ordinary.

There are fewer people at the extreme ends of opinion, who talk in terms of the good or evil of computing. Computer hardware has become a standard budget item like desks and fluorescent lighting. "No one ever got fired," the saying goes, "for buying an IBM computer." As if the decision had only to do with software compatibility and service records. No one ever got smart, either, from mere proximity to a machine of admittedly fine quality but which is as empty of educational content as the next machine in the absence of good software and someone who can apply it well.

As for software, it waltzes into the schools on the coattails of textbooks as auxiliary material — recommended, banal — often in an embarrassed attempt to validate a previous hardware investment. *Spent badly?* (Someone will have egg on their face, left over from the purchase of three dozen computers, half of which don't work and none of which show any signs of fulfilling the original dream.) The answer is often to *spend more*, this time on redemptive software that, of course, can't do the job either. Its increasingly unquestioned function is to fill that particular slot in the budget.

The Trojan Mouse

Our expectations leave us vulnerable to the exhortations of merchandisers, those encyclopedia salesmen of the eighties who claim — and whose claims are often echoed by a chorus of educators and ambitious parents — to have the answer on a disk or inside a plastic box crammed with chips and hot air. "Software in the schools is a Trojan Mouse," says Judah Schwartz, MIT professor of engineering and education. Like the Trojans, we open the gate to the goods, so flattered by attention and persuaded of benefit that we fail to keep up our guard. The danger here is not from ill-will but from a compulsion to fall in love with technology, as with a new girlfriend every week, and thereby lose track of the real business of our lives.

Having agreed, however tacitly, to the premise that computing is necessary, we assume that the more educational computing the better. The nation just can't seem to shake the reflexive notion that more of (you name it) is better: more micros (should they be Apples, IBMs or the luxurious DEC Rainbows?), networks, network systems, and interactive video. The only regret is that, alas, in this time of shrunken, unsubsidized budgets, educators can't have more sooner. Sometimes cross, sometimes plaintive, the cry goes up: there are still not enough machines and accompanying educational software.

Our excessively high opinion of the computer's educational potency is accompanied by a pair of equally false assumptions — that developers can produce high quality software at a rate commensurate with our desire to use it, and that the culture can assimilate the new technology at the same breakneck speed. Computer power in the schools has been doubling at a time when the entire U.S. economy is strained and the schools are in comparably poor financial condition, when almost no good educational software is available, and when neither educators, parents, nor developers know diddly-squat about how to use computers for education.

These shortcomings haven't stopped software developers from going to market full speed ahead. Some have thought they could take various short cuts on the way to a determination of what software to produce. One popular route involves soliciting the opinions of experts in every field from marketing to cognitive psychology. From their theory-driven views are distilled plans for new, improved products. Another route involves assembling a "focus group" — a collection of people, not necessarily expert, drawn at random from sociologically correct populations. This is a market-driven approach. The focus group is sometimes asked to scan the marketplace for holes in the array of available products ("What software would you like that's not there?"), the assumption being these holes are vacuums in need of filling. Or the group reviews products still in market testing. These focus group guinea pigs don't know what they want any more than does the population at large, and their opinions are no more valuable. Our collective experience is insufficient ground for fruitful imagining.

In any case the goal is quick identification of product opportunities that may have no bearing on authentic needs, for these are expressed subtly, if at all, and often in a way unwelcome to merchandisers. It is the too-hasty search that gives us such grotesque products as "manage your meat" software — products that may appear useful only because they didn't exist before or because they meet certain criteria for usefulness, which, if one takes a closer look, make sense only within the paralogic of the product itself. Looking back at the mid-eighties from a wiser vantage point, we're going to be amused and embarrassed and amazed by the list of preposterous things we thought we could do with computers. Today, we should not be amused, especially in the educational realm. We're getting too much too soon. And it's hurting our children, like a weed killer that forces plants to grow in excess of their capacity to support the growth.

Grapes of Wrath

Skewed expectations also put us at the brink of terrible disappointment. Nobody wants to hear this, but a school system which has just spent $20,000 on hardware and raised another $20,000 for software is in a bad spot. There's no way to fulfill that level of investment, because decent software simply does not exist on such a grand scale.

It hardly exists at all. At a recent educational software conference in Denver, dozens of teachers gathered around to hear the results of a year's worth of research into social studies software. They stood there with pencils poised, eager to learn which programs to buy, and the expert obliged them with ten names. Were these ten programs *good* programs, would she say? Did they represent good quality software? Well, no, as it turned out. She admitted after the seminar, though only when pressed, that in recommending the programs she was not saying, "This is good software". She was saying, rather, *"This is software that isn't bad, that isn't too flawed to be useful"*. It didn't bother her that she couldn't muster the kind of enthusiasm — cartwheels! shouts of joy! — one might feel for ten favorite books or record albums. It was as if her generally high hopes for computers in education had lowered her hopes for quality and power in the component parts.

This is happening to us all. Software that is supposed to turn the world around is disappointing us right and left, and *we're not paying attention.* Already schools that three years ago embraced LOGO as *the* language for the under-tens are phasing it out, not because they don't like it but because it costs too much for too little. Others are so disgusted with the available software, and frustrated by their inability to integrate what they have into the normal school program, that their thousands of dollars worth of hardware has begun to collect dust. Yet our distress is something we seem to want to ignore, each teacher and parent harboring the occasional private doubt about the software and the hardware and the revolution to come, while as policy-makers we still insist that everything is fine and that we just need more money, more time, and more expertise.

Most people, for example, are instinctively suspicious and skeptical of artificial intelligence, the prospective ability of machines to think intelligently, and the current hope for computers in education. Ask the man on the street if machines can think and he'll scoff, "Of course not!" Confusion sets in when the issue is clouded, the question pushed a few steps down from AI and closer to what we have now. Asked if machines can teach, the average person will hem and haw and say, "Well, maybe so." We certainly behave as if they could.

A worried father — Mr. N — called Tom one evening to ask what kind of computer he should buy for his daughter. The girl was about to graduate from the ninth and final grade at a nearby private school, but she hadn't done well in her classes and had not been accepted at any "good" schools. Mr. N decided to get her a computer — spend $2000 or $2500, if it took that much — as if the machine had a magical ability to transform a struggling child into a successful learner.

This dad is out of the ordinary only insofar as he has a fair amount of money to spend. But his hopes and expectations are shared by many, many people in this world — most of whom, deep down in their hearts, know better. Surely Mr. N knows how much more effective it would be to spend half of that money on a private tutor, possibly one of the student teachers at his daughter's school. Four hours a day through the summer, even if one of those hours was spent gossiping, would be infinitely more valuable than any machine. Surely we all know better! But we close our eyes and hold our breath like Mr. N. We keep acting as if computers can teach, think, and solve our problems, while we wait for our insincts to quiet down.

This is a set up for bitterness and backlash. The greater the hopes, the deeper the disappointment, and the hopes for educational computing were — and still are in most quarters — about as high as they get. Too high! Too much is expected from the technology! The backlash from those burned is likely to be, almost by definition, reactive, wasteful, blind. Like any overextended group, having spent more money and effort than it can afford to lose, the schools are likely to recoil, twice shy, reluctant to participate further. That would be a terrible loss, for the schools represent not only the largest and most promising arena for the use of computers for education but a major source of feedback to publishers and designers about what is appropriate. It is vital that schools continue to maintain the energy and resources to experiment — loosely, lightly! They must keep trying new ways to integrate computers in the classroom while keeping their educational priorities in clear focus.

The Case of David B

Consider the case of David B, who is a grown man, an artist, with two teen-age children, three cats, and one computer. David's relationship with his computer evolved in a way that may be generalized from the personal to the public realm.

At first, says David, there's terrific excitement. "You're utterly enchanted with the machine and with your own progress in learning new skills."

The second stage is escape. "By diving into the computer, you avoid your problems. Every other part of your life stands still, or so you allow yourself to think. It's not like painting, where you have to confront your emotions in order to do it at all." It was at this stage that David's wife remarked, "You've not been such a good friend since you got that computer." David was incredulous. It took an intervention in the form of a family vote to make him realize how far he'd wandered.

Then he moved on to the stage he describes as integration. "You try to involve the computer in your normal life, by using it to write stories or poetry. But you get tangled up in the technology again in order to make it do what you want it to do."

David eventually grew bored with his computer. He plays around with it now and then, but mainly it serves as another cluttered surface among piles of books and drawings. While he did manage to get through the escape stage, he did not succeed in satisfactorily integrating the machine into his life. In his case, the computer was not terribly important, either in terms of work or play. Its fate was of no particular consequence. But given the magnitude of the matter — the cost and the fact that we're talking about our children's future — the same is not true for computers in the schools. The ever-hopeful coalition of parents, teachers, and others concerned with education is in the thrall of all three stages at once — enchantment, escape, and integration. Though fading, the enchantment is still powerful. Escape into technology is inappropriate, and escape from it is impossible. We're trying in various ways to integrate the stuff, but from a perspective ill-adapted to real needs and capabilities.

As we do our fervent best to embrace a technology that is simultaneously way below our expectations and way beyond our ability to deal with it, we overlook the fact that it might not make sense to transform education quite this way. On the path to educational heaven, educators are becoming alienated from their own visions, software designers and publishers are faltering, and gaps are widening between haves and have nots and between "computer literates" and those who are not. We cannot afford to fail in our efforts to integrate computers appropriately.

The 3-D Revolution

The educational computer revolution must be a three-dimensional phenomenon. It takes hardware — affordable hardware of reasonable quality, that works and is satisfactorily integrated with the other elements of the school program. It takes exciting, interesting, well-designed software. And it takes significant cultural change, a nation getting accustomed to the technology, familiar with its strengths and its weaknesses, and teachers willing and able to make something of it. This is the kind of change that doesn't happen overnight, but slowly, with fits and starts, with one step backward for every two the other way. Since none of its three dimensions have been developed to any great extent, the revolution in education is still little more than an overly-expensive assertion of a vision. Right now it is all dressed up in expectations, waiting in the taxi just at the curb, on its way not to heaven but to where the sellers sell and buyers buy. It does not yet have the critical length, breadth, or depth to support a full-scale alteration in the way children are educated. It is nevertheless sufficiently bulky to crowd our view of what is important in education and to rattle our sense of what makes sense.

It is simply too early to tell what role computers can and should play in education. Neither must we let ourselves get so discouraged that we extinguish all hope. We need a new, shared vision somewhere in between the desolate and the supernal. Something modest that recognizes the social and economic realities that both stimulate and impede the revolution. Something that takes as a given the here and now, the green cinderblock-walled schools that have not, admittedly, been successful, and the homes that can barely afford a winter's worth of oil.

We need to "mess around" with educational computing without agenda or deadlines, with our enchantment kept in moderation and the impulse to escape kept in check. We need to take a look at what is really happening in those schools and consider what we want to have happen — whether, and how, to utilize the technology in the service of our children's education. What we find may be surprising.

3.

Real Life

The great beast slouches toward the schools, spurred by a vo-
ciferous coalition of parents, children, teachers, school administrators, and those segments of the hardware and software
industries that stand to gain some several billion dollars from
pushing educational computing. The members don't always see
themselves as part of a coalition. Indeed, there is considerable
ambivalence among the parties, a reluctance to jump on (or stay
on) a bandwagon shared by groups whose goals do not always
seem compatible. There's a certain helplessness about the movement, each group blaming another for the course. "Yes, we're
in favor of computer education although it's not clear that the
present trend (be it rate of implementation, style of software,
definition of computer literacy, or whatever) is appropriate.
We're doing it this way under pressure from (parents, school
teachers and administrators, the industry")."

Parents of course want their children to have the best possible
education. If the information age is really here, if what is visible
today is just the tip of a technological iceberg that will come
swelling and crashing up into the twenty-first century, then by

golly those kids had better be prepared. It is somewhat moot whether this means that kids should be equipped with a replacement set of skills. ("The skills required in a computer society differ from the traditional reading, writing, and arithmetic skills," — so goes this argument — "and students will need these new skills for employment.") Whether they should add to their current battery the knowledge of how to communicate with the computer and be able to use it for personal and/or professional purposes. Whether their exposure should be to computers as "teachers" of the so-called traditional subjects or as something more transcendental such as an "object-to-think-with." Or whether it is as consumers-to-be — shrewd in their judgment of products, fluent with myriad application programs, wise to the cultural impact of the whole business — that children need training. Who is to know what is really necessary? Who is willing to take any chances? It's like health insurance: one wants to be covered for any eventuality.

The media, the future, the industry, and the kids are leaning on the parents to get with it. So the parents buy the best personal computer they can (or cannot) afford and try mightily to use the thing for educational ends. They fork over $500 they don't have for a cheap computer...and get burned. They get the thing home and immediately discover that since it uses up three electrical outlets — for the monitor, the power supply, and the disk drive — they have to unplug all the lamps in the room. It's late. They don't have a three-way adapter, and all the hardware stores are closed, so they sit there in the dark. Literally. Fooling around with a machine that has come onto the market too fast to have gone through the standard consumer reality checks of the sort that revealed that food processors should have little rubber feet.

We all have certain, well-founded expectations of what a consumer item should be. We expect to take the box home from the store, pry off the staples, take the blender or power drill or whatever it is out from under its styrofoam casing and use it right then and there. If it doesn't work, we take it straight back to the store. Although they're also presented as consumer items, home computers aren't nearly so straightforward. No sooner do we get the lights back on than the thing gets zapped by static and has to go back to the shop. Low-end, so-called affordable home computers are so hypersensitive, and have so many malfunctioning components, that they're "down" more often than not. A toaster oven is about a thousand times more reliable! When they do work their capability is disappointing and their compatibility with other models is almost nil. As many as one in ten U.S. families may own a home computer, but how many of them use it past the first week? How many people at this very moment are still on their hands and knees, searching for the third electrical outlet? How many are too anxious or alienated from the technology to be able to deal with the simplest problems, or in some cases even to recognize they're not getting full value? It is quite possibile to use a computer indefinitely without realizing that it's operating on the equivalent of three cylinders. This combination of consumer inexperience and flaky technology is deadly. The machine gets packed up in a fit of boredom or frustration to languish in the back of the hall closet along with hookahs and fondue pots from the sixties. A $3000 computer is likely to give better service and be less likely to end up in the closet, if only for reasons of vanity. Even so, it may be all but educationally useless since the educational software available for the home does little more than mitigate the guilt of having spent $500 or $3000 on a toy offering no cardiovascular benefits whatsoever.

Of the $1 billion in annual sales of educational software projected for 1987, three-quarters is expected to be of programs for home use. Having recovered from an initial fling with terrible, tedious, bestselling software that promised everything short of a full scholarship to Yale, but provided nothing but expense and boredom, parents are turning to more interesting stuff. What they're buying is fun (it has to be; otherwise it won't be used) and it's practical (some of it) — word processors, spreadsheets, flight simulators. This is nice, but is it education? Is it an alternative to schooling? No. Educational computing in the home is only supplementary to the computer work going on in school. One market opens up the other and vice versa, widening exposure, increasing demand.

Back to School

The fantasy that homes would take the place of schools has not come to pass, due to failure, among other reasons, to recognize the obvious fact that schools are entrenched as institutions of learning. That children are gathered there in groups and thus have a place for the social interaction that is so critical to development and to learning. And that in the school are invaluable resources — books, maps, encyclopedias, and teachers, the greatest resource of all. Homes are not so well equipped to provide a comprehensive learning environment for children. Homes are private worlds, exclusionist and isolated, physically and socially, from each and every other supposed outpost of do-it-yourself heaven. Who is going to stay home with the kids, anyway? Any suggestion that homes take over the job of providing education contains the unspoken assumption that an unpaid mother should take over the job from a paid, and usually female, teacher.

There are something on the order of ten million microcomputers in U.S. homes today, or roughly fifteen times the number in schools. The parents attached to those ten million micros want parallel action in school for their kids. Likewise, parents without computers want schools to provide their kids with the same opportunities enjoyed by the kids who have computers at home. So the parents lean on the school board, campaigning for computers, just as years ago they insisted on the New Math. They support fund raising drives — necessarily so; the high cost requires the backing of local taxpayers in addition to other funding — and are loud in urging that their children's school not be allowed to slip behind the school in the next district. By what measure? By the number of computers in the school. Achieving gains along that index is foremost on parents' agenda. It is not matched in appropriate proportion by consideration for the supporting curriculum or the needs of the instructional staff.

The school's agenda is in many ways parallel. No accident: it is designed to conform to the wishes of the community whose support is vital and whose taste runs to a conservative blend of the measurable new and the known. Principals, as much as parents though for different reasons, want their schools to have what is most modern. They too are swayed by the notion that the future effectiveness of today's students will depend increasingly on their ability to understand computers and to utilize them advantageously. "The revolution caused by computer use presents a critical challenge to education," and so forth. Truancy laws notwithstanding, schools must also compete with television, video, drugs, and other enticements for students' attention. In a line of reasoning reminiscent of the late sixties, when process and currency were in the ascendant, it is feared that if schools don't hop on the bandwagon — if they drag their feet as they did, for instance, about the hand-held calculator — kids will get the message even more clearly than they do already, that schooling is irrelevant. School administrators, like the parents, are measuring value in terms of the number of micros in the school and the number of students enrolled in the computer literacy course. This focus on counting is again given precedence over teacher training and the larger curriculum questions.

What are schools getting in their high-priced bid for heaven? More than 85 percent now have at least one microcomputer, but no more than a third of the students in any school get to use the computer. Ever. It may be just as well, given the flimsiness of school computers. They're nothing like those Bell & Howell projectors from the fifties that were so tough one could practically stir paint with them, or those solid, hard plastic school microscopes with enormous knobs and a nice dust cover. Get chalk in the disk drive of a school computer and you're done for, class is dismissed. Everyday static — the kind kids whip up to stick balloons to their hair — will wipe out huge chunks of memory. Power spurts (common in almost every urban setting), excessive heat, magnetic fields, and jarring (ditto) can also be damaging. Many machines have faulty on/off switches. One popular model is so poorly designed that picking up just the disk drive, instead of the whole computer, lets the guts of the machine come spilling out in a terrifying mass of chips and ribbon cable.

Software? Applications? Schools these days are waiting for comprehensive software curricula spanning kindergarten through grade twelve. Meanwhile, the individual packages are gushing out into the market — six or seven million units purchased in 1985; tens of thousands of different programs to teach foreign languages, math, geography, song writing, business operations, life-coping skills. The programs are fussy — they balk at one false move — and most programs are so badly designed one feels caught in a sort of twilight zone between garbage and gorgeous technology. At least 90 percent of the educational software on the market is not worth buying.

As for teachers, they're doing remarkably well under the circumstances. When microcomputers were first introduced in the schools, beginning around 1981, the assumption was that teachers would be threatened. Under the circumstances, it would not have been surprising if they had crept into school at night and smashed the machines into tiny pieces, for computers were introduced amid much fanfare about how they would soon replace the teachers who had so badly let us down. The kids were excited, of course, because they're young and like that arcade parlor sort of thing. But teachers? Teachers were known to be conservative, set in their ways. They were expected to be anxious about losing their jobs and fearful to the point of paralysis about learning how to use the computers in the classroom.

It hasn't turned out that way at all. In fact, many teachers have turned their hearts and souls to stimulating the development of educational computing in the schools. They have gone to computer conferences, bought their own machines, and plowed through hopelessly inarticulate manuals to learn how to use them. But only a small handful of teachers in the schools that have computers have had an opportunity to use the things to much purpose. In about half the micro-owning schools, according to a nationwide Johns Hopkins survey, only one or two teachers at the most are regular users. Limited access and lack of training have combined to keep even rudimentary use within the province of a select few. For these few, the computer offers escape from monotony and a gimmicky means to satisfy the public relations goals of their bosses, the principals and school administrators.

Closing the Circle

The hardware and software industries have been instrumental in convincing parents, educators, and the general public of the necessity of computers in education. As the home market for computers collapses — due to saturation, backlash, and the inevitable fall relative to an overly high aim — manufacturers intensify pressure on the schools to pick up the slack. They are guilty of exploiting the insecurities of their audience, for schools on the edge of hysteria about the coming age are primed to buy anything that promises to get them ready. It's like selling a defective casket to a not-rich widow in the throes of her grief. "With all this pressure," writes educator Alan Neibauer in the *Technological Horizons in Education Journal, (T.H.E.),* "the public is supporting the unchecked expenditure of public funds, the growing wedge between classes of students, and the waste of student energy and talents."

The industry has managed to convince the schools that they not only bear the heaviest responsibility for teaching kids about computers, but that they're also vaguely guilty of not doing more sooner. It is under these conditions that schools accept computers that fall apart in class or quality machines that blow the budget. Apple, Commodore, IBM, Tandy, Atari, even Digital and AT&T are offering fantastic discounts to educators. They're giving the stuff to schools by the truckload, providing faculty seminars and what they take liberty to call educational software. They do this in full recognition of the fact that each computer in a school is a bundle of sales potential radiating out like the rings from a stone dropped in a pond — sales not only of software and peripheral equipment but of computers to the parents as well.

Here the circle closes, for the schools in their turn lean on the software industry — on publishers and independent developers — to produce the educational software they need to validate their current investment and to satisfy the demands of the community for tip-top (that is to say, computerized) education. Understandably enough, the educational software industry does what it has to do to make money. It floods the home market with games billed as educational yet fun enough to hold the attention of an audience that doesn't have to play if it doesn't want to. And it cranks out what the schools will pay for, which at this point in our history is fairly dry stuff, ancillary to textbooks and promising the measurable results so highly valued in the move back to basics.

Market projections in early 1985 put the number of microcomputers in schools by 1987 at somewhere near two million.

The price would be $7 billion. The educational software market, which jumped in one year from $100 to $200 million in 1984, has been expected to continue this annual doubling to clear $1 billion by 1987. We don't know enough about what to do with educational computing to spend this kind of money. Already there are doubts, failures, and disappointments as current sellers struggle for position in the education marketplace. Hardware companies are doing badly — falling profits, layoffs, closeouts. The tremendous proliferation of software manufacturers in the late 1970s and early 1980s is being brought to a near halt by an industry shakeout, the results of which can be seen in the form of price-slashed software in Sears' bargain bins and hundreds of hopeful young design companies either throwing in the towel or entertaining offers to be bought, for cheap, by big corporations. The *Boston Globe* set the tone in mid-March 1985, just two short years and a couple of months after *Time* named the personal computer "Machine of the Year": "More and more, it's beginning to look as though [this] is not going to be the year of the computer." It appears that the eighties, that sparkling decade we hoped would be decorated with personal computers for all, is instead the scene of corporate turf wars and a small-scale game of educational musical chairs.

Bringing In the Hardware

In the fall of 1980, which is as good a date as any for when it all began, there were approximately 31,000 microcomputers available for instructional use in U.S. schools. Tripling every eighteen months, the number had jumped to 97,000 by the spring of 1982 and to 325,000 by August 1984. These are conservative, U.S. Department of Education statistics. Other estimates put the 1984 figure as high as one million. The Johns Hopkins survey found that as of January 1983, 53 percent of all U.S. schools had obtained at least one microcomputer for instructional use. A more recent study, conducted by John F. Hood of Market Data Retrieval, found that, as of the fall of 1984, 85.1 percent of all schools had a microcomputer. Secondary schools on their own registered 77 percent in 1983 and climbing; elementary schools were at 42 percent, or roughly where secondary schools were two years previous. Forty percent of secondary schools had five or more microcomputers, though only 7 percent of elementary schools did so; 10 percent of secondary schools had their micros linked in some kind of network.

What to do, oh what to do, with these splendid machines? Here is a collection of fashionable notions — impractical, contradictory, yet already inflated to the status of truth — that have dictated how computers are being used in the schools. Computer-wise educators debate them with the passion of those who have already experienced the consequences of inappropriate computer use in schools.

> *Comfy Is As Comfy Does* – Put the computer in a nice, friendly room, with plants and posters and comfy chairs (in other words, create an ideal children's bedroom in the school) in order to make the computer more accessible, especially to those who might be intimidated by its seemingly hard edges. Keep it away from the chaotic classroom, which has its own business to attend to and an entire social structure to maintain. The computer is a thing apart that needs, like an infant, a little coddling, a little TLC.

> *Face the Music* – Put the computer in the math lab where it belongs. The fact of the matter is that it's the math wizards who want to use it, and they're also the ones who know how to use it, so don't fight it. Already they can do more things with the computer than the teacher dreamed possible. These kids are the programmers of the future, and the bigger their head start, the better off we'll be.

> *Closed-door Policies* – Do not make the mistake of putting the computer in the math lab. Sure it's a separate room and it may be the only separate room available, but its liabilities vastly outweigh its assets. A computer in the math lab will instantly become the exclusive province of a tiny handful of brainy kids, who were already antisocial (and frankly, a little weird) and will now withdraw even further. Off they'll go into computerland, and the

rest of the kids won't be able to get so much as a foot in the door.

A Separate Peace – Do not put the computer in a corner of the classroom, because one kid will dominate the machine and upset everyone else. There he'll be (the kid will almost certainly be a *he*), lost in the world of the machine, deaf to the teacher and all else around him. Heaven only knows what he's learning, if anything; the teacher has the rest of the class to contend with. Meanwhile, the kid will be shouting hysterically, jumping up and down in front of the terminal and generally spilling into everyone else's consciousness. It can be quite distracting. One might think his enthusiasm would spread to other kids, and it does occasionally, but they will have to wait their turn.

Networking for Kids – Try to get as many terminals as possible, so each child can have a turn. Better yet, get a lot of terminals and link them together in a networking system in one big room. You can bring the kids in batches, sit each one down in front of his or her terminal, give the whole lot of them their drill-and-practice, and march them out again. It's much easier to administer this way.

Wholistic Computing – Whatever you do, don't buy into a rigid networking system. These systems demand a huge commitment of time and attention simply to be kept in working order. The service contract alone is a significant budget item, and additional time and attention is required for system operation. Some networked schools have even found it necessary to hire a software librarian. Instead, immerse yourself and your kids in a more naturally computer-rich learning environment. The computers need not be tightly networked. A loose, almost random arrangement is preferable. It's best if computers are available to any and all children, regardless of their perceived interests or learning styles. Children who are interested in "soft" subjects — art, writing, and so forth — will find as many delightful ways to use the machines as will those who are oriented toward math and other "hard" subjects.

Contradictory though these positions might be, they have in common a certain cart-before-the-horse quality, a hardware-drivenness that tries to fit the situation — the classroom, the kids, the lessons — to the technology. Educators stand firm on one position or another as they dash about like Don Quixote into the future. Each argument is compelling, for it contains an element of truth. Each argument also carries with it certain financial and educational implications which, if multiplied times all the schools in the country would begin to add up. Most are insupportably expensive. Some may be financially manageable by an individual school but so contrary to the natural rhythms of the school as to doom the local future of educational computing. Not only is the data yet unavailable that would have to go into a broad prescription, the answer must be different for each situation.

Boston (in real life) chose to get quite enthusiastic about computers, raising $4 million in the early 1980s — from the City of Boston during the height of a fiscal crisis, from the School Department, and from the private sector — to bring computers into the schools. They bought 2500 micros for 50,000 students, making Boston, at 1:20, second in the nation (Broward County, Florida, is first) in the ratio of microcomputers to kids. The current number of micros, the product of a massive drive, is unlikely to increase in the near future, for no federal funds are coming through and state funds have slowed to a trickle. This is true for other school systems as well. The money has stopped.

Those other systems are not so well endowed as the city across the river from MIT and ringed by what is known as "America's Technology Highway." The national average is one micro for every 90 to 100 students, with distribution following the usual inequitable patterns. Southern parochial and rural schools, schools in the low socio-economic brackets, and schools serving predominately minority populations are much less likely to have computers than their "better-off" counterparts. How these schools use the computers they have is a separate matter, but similarly loaded with questions about fairness and equitable distribution of computer technology. And the gap is widening; growth does not mean equity. Schools that already have computers are more likely to buy additional units than those who have none are likely to buy their first.

Making Good

The money is raised and the hardware is in place, not as abundantly as one might wish, but better than nothing, perhaps. The focus on hardware has served a dual purpose. It has driven us to consume the perfect consumer item, one of those major investments that immediately call for further investment in supporting technology, furniture, accessories, program material. And, by being so very engaging (one could spend months, for example, in comparison shopping for the perfect 180 characters-per-second printer for under $1000), it has shielded us from the matter of just what on God's green earth we expect to accomplish.

Here's another collection of fashionable notions about educational applications of the technology. They are as contradictory as those having to do with how to handle the machines. They have been similarly instrumental in shaping the course of computer use in the schools.

> *A Kid's Best Friend* – Give each child a set of computer-aided lessons and let her study on her own, alone with the machine, at whatever pace is comfortable. Remember, this is the first generation to grow up with computers, and most of these kids are already quite at ease with the concepts, if not with the details of programming and hardware. Well-designed computerized lessons (the ones called "student-proof" are the most robust) provide complete, individualized instruction as well as word processing capability for note-taking, a dictionary to prevent misspelling, and help menus should any questions arise about how to use the program. The kids can't screw it up (and neither can the

teacher), no matter how hard they try. Most importantly, computerized lessons free the teacher to spend time with other children, on the material that still requires personal attention.

Stick to the Knitting – Be sure you understand that the computer was designed as a tool for mathematical computation. Its roots go back at least as far as the abacus, that early hand-held decimal calculator, although Blaise Pascal (1623-1662) usually gets credit for building the first machine (the "Pascaline") that could add and subtract. British mathematician Charles Babbage (1792-1871) is known as the Father of the Computer for his (never finished) work on an "analytical engine" which, with the help of Lady Ada Lovelace, could theoretically do nifty things like looping and subroutines and conditional jumps. Despite valiant efforts to give it broad-spectrum application, the computer of today is still essentially a math tool, and should be used as such — to do math and to teach math.

The Universal Substance – Don't give kids the message that computers are just for math, for nothing could be further from the truth. Computers have virtually unlimited application in all areas of modern life, from psychology to art to space exploration. The best thing you can do for children is to give them a firm grounding in how to use the computer. Teach them BASIC, of course, plus one of the other higher level languages such as Pascal or C. Once they have some programming skills, they can do just about anything.

Everything in Its Place – Hold firm against the onslaught of arcade-style educational software and against the more insidious pressure to make learning "fun" and "motivating." We do our children no service by extending to the schools the hyper-fun culture of the streets and the media. Learning games and other such contrivances may, in fact, be incompatible with learning, which is, necessarily, serious business. There can be no room for this fluff in a curriculum committed to the basics.

There is room for software, yes indeed, but software
that reflects proven pedagogical methods and can demonstrate no-nonsense skill gain.

Again, these opinions about educational applications propel
their various advocates hither and yon, forming the basis for
decisions that have massive impact on our kids, our schools, and
the software industry. Just as it is wise to remember that no one
path is the correct one when it comes to bringing in the hardware, it makes sense to stay equally loose with software.

What Color Is Your Elephant?

One blind man sees a thick rope, another a fearsome arching
spear, as they each grab hold of various features of the thing
they do not know is an elephant. The other blind men see still
different things — a blanket, a tree, a wall, and a snake — or
so the story goes. The computer is likewise viewed as however
many things there are people looking at it. It is listed among
that group known as instructional aids, of which flash cards and
slide projectors are more pedestrian members. It is an "object-
to-think-with" like Cuisenaire Rods or the differential gear systems that inspired the young Papert to turn to mathematics with
wonder and love. It is a post-industrial piece of chalk, a transcendental combo of pencil and scissors and glue, a playmate as
fun as a barrel of monkeys with knowledge up its harlequin
sleeves, a ticket off the unemployment line of the twenty-first
century. It is to be recognized as a cultural phenomenon, something one should be informed about. It is to be appreciated,
like music or art; one is thought to be the better person for
knowing about RAM and ROM. It is that most current of psy-
choanalytical morsels, the transitional object, like the baby blanket clung to long past its prime by a child with one-and-a-half
feet out the nursery door.

"The computer sits on many borders," writes Turkle. She
describes it as potentially a bridge between formal scientific
thought and the softer, fuzzier, intuitive style of thinking commonly understood as "feminine" but which one, male or female,

must unavoidably practice in inventing formal systems. It is in some views a transitional object to mediate relationships between people and machines, and math, and other people. It is, like the primordial clay now thought by some scientists and fundamentalist Christians to be the original stuff of life, a magnet for energy and imagination, for controversy, fantasy, fear, and high hope.

Schools engaged in educational computing are grappling with a very evocative elephant indeed. Confronted by these myriad possibilities and the various dictates of fashion, they have chosen a thousand different ways to proceed. Objectives range from getting acquainted ("getting over the fear" is how it's sometimes put, although children have no natural fear of computers — or math or particle physics, for that matter — only what is cultivated) to having full command of a computer language. For the purpose of examining what is going on in schools, let us employ the Henry Olds' software classification system. In the first category, the computer is used as a delivery vehicle for the teaching of the same skills and concepts that were taught in the pre-computer era. In the second category, the thing to be learned is the computer itself, along with an assortment of cognitive skills thought to spin off directly from exposure to the technology. In the third category, the computer is used to create environments where learning can be more effective and more social.

The Computer as an Instructional Medium The short form here is CAI, or computer-aided instruction. CAI represents the most common and most maligned use of computers in education. As the form that most closely parallels the public image of traditional teaching methods, it is easily understood by a public just beginning to get the hang of what computers are all about. It is also the easiest (therefore the cheapest) type of software to design, and the most readily evaluated.

The CAI category includes drill-and-practice software and tutorials. Drill-and-practice programs use the computer as a glorified set of flash cards to help the student go over material already learned in the hope of getting it better. The subject matter covered — math, spelling, vocabulary, foreign languages, typing — is unambiguous and tightly defined; one is either right or wrong in answering the questions. A good score will often solicit a reward in the form of praise ("well done!") or reinforcing sound effects and flashing images on the screen. A low score is sometimes remarked by insults ("you turkey!"), although most drill-and-practice programs are set to give the right answer after a number of tries, to relieve frustration. A student can use these infinitely patient programs at his or her own pace, and can choose the most appropriate among a range of levels of instructional difficulty.

Tutorials use the computer as a private teacher (a *good* teacher, Olds notes, is the implicit assumption) to provide direct instruction in a skill or subject. The well-motivated student can learn the new material from the basics on up, working through one step at a time, taking periodic quizzes to check progress — and all this without outside help. As with drill-and-practice, the content of tutorials is clearly specified. One answer for each question is generally assumed to be correct, with a beginning as unambiguous as the start of the Olympic hurdles and a self-paced path to the designated finish composed of discreet, bite-sized pieces of information, which added together in sequence are supposed to form knowledge. One can study geography this way, or math or typing or accounting procedures, as well as a slew of job-related skills. The best tutorials adjust to the learner's growing understanding, although most are still simply a portion of a textbook transferred to disk.

The Computer as a Tool   General-purpose tools include word processing and database management programs. Financial spreadsheets, sometimes classified as simulations, have more in common with the general-purpose tools since they do not have built-in rules. The user establishes his own rules — the formula for advertising rates, for example, and the relationship between X inventory and projected sales of Y. The computer is used here like any other tool would be, to help people carry out tasks within a general application area — to write with freedom from uncorrectable mistakes and to "crunch" numbers with such ease that one can focus on the meaning of the numbers, not the labor. Learning to use these tools, as once we learned to use a slide rule, is an important part of our children's education.

A program is a special-purpose tool if its task is more narrowly defined. A spelling checker is such a tool, as are the numerous business-related programs for accounts receivable, inventory control, payroll, and so forth. Special-purpose tools in education are generally used for administrative purposes such as keeping grade records and scheduling classes.

Computers are used also as tool-making tools, to create general- and special-purpose tools of one's own design. All computer languages can be so classified. Programming is thus the process of making tools to help one do something else — animate graphics, create drill-and-practice programs, regulate the Hoover Dam. Among the most exciting possibilities is use of the computer to create the intellectual tools best suited to one's particular needs and purposes — a custom "notebook," for example, in which to record observations or events according to certain cross-referenced themes, or a program to follow the movement of stars observable from one's own backyard. Some computer tools are silly; some are marginally useful; and some, such as word processors and spreadsheets, are so terrific that users often wonder how they ever lived without them.

The Computer as a Modeling Device Learning games and simulations comprise the third group. They have in common the use of the computer to model an interactive environment, whether purely imaginary or based on reality, in which the student is challenged to learn in the course of maneuvering in and out of that environment. Anything that can be taught via CAI can be taught through games and simulations. More, for this kind of software also involves the student in learning-intense interactions, with the computer and with other people, and that in itself can be instructive.

Games are generally described as "fun" and often feature arcade-style action, snappy graphics, and sound effects in addition to the instructional content. The fun part is understood to be motivating, which in turn is understood to be beneficial to the learning process, although there rages among the specialists a somewhat baffling debate as to whether fun and learning are compatible. That aside for the moment, games tend to fall along a spectrum ranging from those in which instruction predominates (CAI in disguise) to those which offer genuinely fun-filled, long-lived play, but whose educational content is harder to pin down.

Computer-based or otherwise, a simulation is a model of reality. It is by definition not an exact copy; neither is it a duplicate
or mirror-image, but a metaphor, rather, of some aspect of
reality that is sufficiently large and complex to be worth exploring yet amenable to manipulation. Games are also simulations, though often less metaphorically literal. Monopoly is a
simulation of the world of high finance. Pac-Man is set in a
simulated maze inhabited by monsters and a legless yellow om-
nivore whose sustenance is "dots" and whose trump card is a
cache of energy cookies. Students entering these metaphorical
environments are free to play "what if?" games — to explore,
experiment, and experience the consequences of their actions
without real-world risk. They can take the role of another person to gain an often enlightening perspective, and they can
experiment with the many interwoven variables that are the
fabric of the simulation. Understanding gained through the
simplified model is supposed to lead to better understanding of
the complex reality.

Hovering above the scene like the Goodyear blimp is "computer literacy," an umbrella term with so many different mean-
ings as to be virtually meaningless and which, by appropriating
a term previously reserved for reading and writing the common
language, yanks itself up by the bootstraps to an impressive but
false stature. At first, in the initial 1981-1983 flurry, computer
literacy was generally defined as the understanding of how computers work, how they function. Since 1983, the popular definition has shifted to mean a user's facility with applications
programs such as word processing and the like, or familiarity
with a computer language. In some schools the latter qualifies
for foreign language credit.

As of late 1984, eleven states nationwide included something
called computer literacy among high school graduation requirements, but the programs are often inadequately defined and
insupportable as an official educational requirement. New
Hampshire, for example, requires such a course but lacks parallel certification requirements for computer teachers. Some
New Hampshire districts, especially those with low tax bases,
are so strapped for funds that they are being forced to consol-
idate with neighboring districts in order to support the new

program. Two other states have a computer literacy requirement for teachers and administrators, and a dozen others plan
to include such a requirement for certification. The term remains utterly vague and as many-sided as the elephant.

Up Close and Personal

In real life (as measured by the Johns Hopkins survey), only
one student in seven, in the schools that have a computer, uses
the machine for any purpose in a typical week. Elementary
schools generally favor giving access to as many students as
possible, with the result that the average user gets to use the
computer less than thirty minutes per week; one-third get it for
fifteen minutes or less. Drill-and-practice is the preferred activity in elementary schools. While a few children use the computer, the rest of the class (what to do with them is always a
problem) are doing seatwork. Whole-class lectures or discussions
are avoided when the computer is in use.

Programming takes the lead in secondary schools, along with
computer literacy, which is sometimes programming, sometimes
drills, sometimes "getting acquainted." Secondary schools on the
average favor longer use by fewer numbers of students. Result:
the majority of students who use the computer do so for forty-
five minutes or more per week. The typical programming student uses a micro for nearly an hour every week, but the student
using the computer for skills practice gets only seventeen minutes per week. Does an hour of programming sound like a lot?
It is, relatively, but very little programming can actually be done
in an hour. Computer-based simulations and learning games
are used regularly in about one-fifth of schools with micros.
Even with eight computers in the classroom, a luxury shared by
less than 20 percent of secondary schools, students may spend
as much as three-quarters of the allotted time waiting for their
turn at the computer.

Experienced secondary schools, with a few years of computing
behind them, are increasingly inclined to teach *about* computers
— how to program, how to use pre-programmed applications
packages — than to use them to help teach basic skills. It may

be that these pioneering schools have already given up computer-aided instruction as wasteful. Their disenchantment
would not be surprising, for the upper grades have been getting
the least of what is universally agreed is a bad lot. Most school-
oriented software goes to the lower grades, apparently under
the assumption that, since younger kids have to choke down a
wad of rules, facts, and skills in order to get off the ground,
then the more efficiently they can do that the better. Very little
comes to the secondary school. David Thornburg, associate editor of *COMPUTE!*, found that only 2 percent of educational
software for school or home is directed to teenagers. LOGO,
which need not be so confined, has not crossed over to the older
children, and no comparably exciting educational computing
environment has been devised for them.

This is how it looks up close. In a typical microcomputer-
owning elementary school, two micros are used eleven hours
apiece by 16 percent of the kids (64 in a student body of 400).
Each kid gets twenty minutes use per week. Forty percent of
that meager time goes to drill-and-practice of math and language facts, spelling, and other items to be memorized. A third
of the time is spent having students copy, write, and test computer programs; the rest on learning games which, especially in
elementary school, are no more than drill-and-practice programs painted red and dressed up with a few guns and bogey-
people.

A typical microcomputer-owning high school has five micros,
each used on the average of thirteen hours per week. This time
is shared among 11 percent of the students (that's 80 kids in a
school of 700) who each spend about forty-five minutes with a
computer in an average week. What are they doing? Two-thirds
of the time is spent on programming and computer literacy
activities and another 18 percent on drill-and-practice, though
it should be noted that despite the percentages there are actually
more hours devoted to drill-and-practice in secondary than in
elementary schools because there are more computers in secondary schools and more time spent on them total. The re-
maining time is split between learning games and various applications activities such as word processing and business-related
programs.

Just as the hardware is unevenly distributed among racial and socio-economic groups, so are the applications. While affluent suburban schools tend to teach their predominately white upper-middle class students how to program — how to tell the computer what do do, in other words — schools serving predominately minority populations concentrate on CAI. These children learn to do what the computer tells them. The Johns Hopkins survey revealed further distinctions within the low income ("low SES") category. In minority communities, the schools with micros use them to raise achievement levels of their lower-performing students, apparently in the belief that drill-and-practice will do what it claims to do — motivate students, provide individualized instruction, teach. In white, low SES communites, however, schools prefer to give access to the higher achievers, teaching them programming, allowing them independently to master computing skills. The assumption here seems to be that slower learners require teacher attention for which the computer is no substitute.

This distinction is confirmed by various observers who note that above-average students have gained the most from the introduction of computers in the school. What wobbly definitions there are of computer literacy tend to be skewed in favor of high achievers, who provide a better showcase of benefits gained. Suburban computer class has become the site of a uniquely middle-class vocational education, producing what will presumably become employable high-technocrats. Minority students and low achievers (with a few shining exceptions such as young Marlon) are left with the drab prospect of becoming the technopeasants of the future.

Back to Basics

The three convergent forces that are pushing computers on the schools — parents, the schools themselves, and the technology industry — have lately been moving "back to basics," that favorite theme now accompanied by the high-priced drone of mass-market software. This movement has sent software back to pedagogical forms so conservative and so lacking in imagination as to render the software virtually useless as anything other than an item to buy and sell.

In a majority of states, adoption boards decide which textbooks are to be used in public schools statewide. Naturally, this arrangement has a significant influence on publishers who stand to gain (or lose) tremendous amounts of money depending on the fate of their textbook series. It is an inducement to comply to the demands of the boards. Many adoption boards now call for comprehensive software packages as ancillaries to the textbooks. There is less concern than ever for the pedagogical merits of this software, only that it be linked to the textbooks. There is less concern also for educational innovation. Writes Papert, "The computer revolution has scarcely begun, but it is already breeding its own conservatism." It is too great a risk for a political organization to entrust the minds of every child in the state of Texas or California or wherever to a radical new approach to teaching basic skills. Games? Simulations? Not acceptable to an institution that does not view play as significant to learning, at least not within the formal constraints of a back-to-basics curriculum.

This is the age of accountability, where educational activities are appraised in terms of their quantifiable results. Education is divided into an increasingly standardized set of learning units, each with specified goals and objectives, and children receive these educational units as they would so many teaspoonsful of medicine, in full knowledge of what is expected of them. In the end they are subjected to an "objective" evaluation; the results (quantified) are understood as evidence of their achievement.

This style is of course not unique to education, but derives from our handling of the natural sciences, which seem to lend themselves to endless subdivision. "The by-product of the great achievement of science," wrote philosopher Jacques Barzun in the *Atlantic Monthly*, "is that everybody's mind is now shaped from the cradle to the grave to trust analysis exclusively."

> The purpose of analysis is to show what little things big things are made of and how the little bits fit together to produce the whole. The only difficulty is to decide what the bits are and when one has got hold of every separate kind. Right now

nuclear physicists seem to be finding an endless series of bits. They tag them as they go and agreement prevails as to their real existence. This is what makes their work *science*.

We have adapted these methods for education, subjecting knowledge to the narrow scrutiny of analysis, chopping it up into little bits with the false confidence that when those bits are known they can be reconfigured into comprehensible wholes. We have embraced the computer in the same spirit. All ones and zeros and chambered data, it seems the perfect vehicle for compartmentalized information and the perfect tool for measuring achievement of prespecified objectives. We cling to the hope of hard, simple evidence notwithstanding every indication that the effects of learning, via computers or otherwise, are as complex and elusive as the effects of a good book.

We don't want to hear about the unknowable, the untestable. We want results, so we go for "wrap-around" software offering guaranteed results on the coattails of textbooks for kindergarten through grade twelve. Educational software for the schools is increasingly of this type, for it fulfills what are perceived as the most pressing goals. Here is one leading brand described in advertising literature:

> Complete computer-aided instruction systems for schools, from kindergarten through high school. Includes
>
> • comprehensive basics curriculum ("The Reading Series teaches children both how to read, and how to understand what they read.");
>
> • administrative and testing software (It tells you what other same-brand software will help the most.); and
>
> • a networked system of student learning stations.

Wrap-around software is clearly and explicitly fitted to the existing curriculum. It dovetails the textbooks chapter by chapter, providing reinforcement and periodic quizzes and requiring thereby, at least superficially, very litte teacher training or initiative. It is basic — overnight it has become fundamental — not a supplementary frill for which, with all the counting and getting back to basics, there is no time or money. Wrap-around software is drill-and-practice because drill-and-practice can most readily be designed, and demonstrated, to run parallel to the textbooks. Wrap-around software is very focused, each unit zeroing in on a single cognitive skill or a tight little cluster of facts. And — the pay-off — wrap-around software produces quantifiable results. It can be demonstrated that children have gained in skills and knowledge and thus, that they have learned.

The production and promotion of K through 12 software is a defensive move by publishers who, recognizing that profits from the school market derive from textbooks, are scrambling to do what they must to please the textbook buyers — the school boards and the state-level adoption boards. They need an adequate return on investment like any other enterprise, but they can't get that these days by being creative. The development of imaginative software takes resources they don't have any more, not since the late sixties federal money dried up and the booming late seventies turned to bust as venture capital withdrew from a market which didn't seem as promising as it once had. Little choice remains but to follow the textbooks, using the computer in the most conventional, unimaginitive ways.

Not that they want to do it. Publishers are book people; they don't know software. And software is so very hard to develop, so expensive, such a pain in the butt. If a book manuscript is flawed, the editor can fix it, but there's nothing he can do on his own to fix a software program with problems. Even a professional software manager, who is often brought in from far away at great cost and inconvenience, may not be able to cure the ailing program.

If a program is fine in the publishing offices, it may not be fine elsewhere. Every disk sent to schools is a time bomb ready to explode at any minute into obsolescence and/or a wriggling mass of bugs. Every disk must be supported, updated, accompanied by the ceaseless handholding known as customer support. Publishers don't want to do it but they have to — like a would-be supplier of a big company might take executives on a weekend hunting trip to Minnesota in order to clinch a big contract. Wrap-around software is now a necessary business expense (they often give the stuff away), a bargaining chip to sell textbooks. They need it quick, and they'll pay for it. Millions. Pay either to develop it in-house or to have it done by any number of the all-too-willing band of software developers who will, for a million or so, pump out software unencumbered by the need to be either profitable or of good quality. Publishers and developers both understand that the function of this software is to sell textbooks.

Imagine the ultimate product — a textbook series plus software wrapped around every last chapter. A complete package in twenty-four volumes, with vinyl covers and molded plastic holders for the diskettes, for sale for $14,000 to every school system in the universe. Publishers think they can sell that kind of package by way of their standard sales approach, which calls for direct mail promotions followed by personal selling. While it would be too expensive to send a rep all the way out to Farmingdale for a $49 sale, $14,000 is another matter. Such is the trend, at any rate, given the pressure on schools to computerize, the market within which educational publishers must operate, and the likelihood of publishers finding software developers willing to undertake the task. This trend is intensified by the tightening of market constraints and with it the shakeout of even moderately well-capitalized manufacturers and publishers. Only the hardy will survive, and they're banking on wraparound systems.

The Big Chill

In the face of tremendous financial and social pressure to computerize education, schools are tentatively responsive to such a neat solution. They want to spend big; they feel they have to spend big — to stay ahead, to satisfy parents who want their kids to stay ahead, and to validate the investment they've already made. But while the pressure continues unabated, disappointment has already set in. Curriculum packages are not fitting neatly into what schools call "promising practices" — the lingo for good programs put to good use. Few such promising practices are likely to emerge so long as the price of the software remains high and the quality low. There is no indication that the cost will decline in any way comparable to the dropping cost of hardware. Labor-intensive as the development process necessarily is, the cost is likely, if anything, to go up. The rare school that can afford a multi-thousand-dollar software system may not have enough machines to go around or the trained teachers to handle the stuff or a curriculum so flexible as to accomodate such a major alteration.

Even if the environmental conditions were such that a K through 12 program could be supported, it may not be what we really want. Given that in the last five years very little educational software has emerged that would constitute a significant subset of any curriculum, it is far from certain that even fifteen or twenty years will be sufficient time to produce quality courseware for an entire curriculum.

The awful truth is that K through 12 software is impossible to do right. If educational software is to be more than a silicon stamp on existing mediocrity — if each lesson, each game, each hour's worth of software is to be truly learning-intense — then the demands of development exceed by far the resources of any earth-bound publisher. The world's ten best designers working around the clock for twenty years couldn't produce enough good software to satisfy current demands. Four thousand frictionless monkeys snorting pure oxygen at state-of-the-art consoles in a Class 100 environment couldn't do the job! It would take not only superhuman effort but an understanding of the computer's role in education that is as yet, necessarily, undeveloped.

Wrap-around software is a disservice both to education and to computers. It further rigidifies a school curriculum already full of artificial barriers between subjects, and institutionalizes a failure to imagine creative roles for computers that could, if handled in other ways, have the opposite effect of breaking down those barriers. Locked into textbooks and the dullest of teaching methods, it squeezes out creative roles for the teacher who could, if allowed more flexibility, choose to use, or not use, computers in more appropriate ways. It is paced but not personal, not readily adaptable to individual classroom situations. And it costs far too much for what it delivers.

In making a major investment in curriculum systems — hardware, software, workbooks, manuals, training — schools risk locking themselves out of valuable advances yet to come. It is an inappropriately rigid posture in this time of flux. Moreover, it is unlikely to reflect an effective or realistic use of current resources. This is not the way to go if we want to make something of computers in education. Along this road we could turn the computer lab into the audio-visual lab of the eighties — an expensive dinosaur which flourished too briefly, and with too little gain, to redeem its high price.

One teacher recently asked the school janitor to remove the television from her classroom, as it was no longer being used for educational purposes. Educators Horace Gordon, David Roberts, and Michael Milone, who recounted this story in a 1984 article in *Academic Therapy*, tell us that as the janitor carried the TV out the door, he turned to the teacher and said, "I was here when they took the radios out."

The computer could join that list of technological marvels that, when all was said and done, did virtually nothing of educational significance, serving only to promote the flow of money and enthusiasm into and then, quickly, out of the schools. "Experience should...make us wary," writes Harvard University president Derek Bok, "of dramatic claims for the impact of the new technology."

> Thomas Edison was clearly wrong in declaring that the phonograph would revolutionize education. Radio could not make a lasting impact on the public schools even though foundations gave generous subsidies to bring programs into the classroom. Television met a similar fate in spite of glowing predictions heralding its powers to improve learning.

Let's not let that happen to computers. Computers are undeniably an important part of our world — so much so that we need to take great care not to bungle the job of incorporating them into the schools. It's a fine line we have to walk. We must not make such a mess at the outset that schools will want to forget the whole thing and retreat back into the dark ages. Neither must we be so foolish as to think we know exactly how to proceed. So let's not yank the schools in yet another ill-considered direction, pumping them full of unsupportable technology only to let it falter in a few years and be packed away as a reminder of time wasted and money poured down the drain.

And let us not subject our children to curricula made ever more rigid by the superimposition of technology. That technology could be turned to modest advantage if we can refrain from institutionalizing its use before we're ready. And if we have the patience to invent new and perhaps counterintuitive ways to use it. Let us do this in mind of what has to be our ultimate goal — the thoughtful, thorough education of our children.

4.

In Search of the Most Amazing Thing

The most amazing thing is a well-educated child. A child who can go forth into the world, confident and joyful in her knowledge of the culture, of how things work and how they came to be that way, receptive to ideas, to art and feeling, skillful at communicating and well-grounded in the habits of acting upon the world, whatever her sphere might be, in decent, equitable, creative, constructive ways. In the search for this amazing thing, educators would be wise to focus on three priorities: literacy, culture, and social skills.

Literacy

True literacy is the ability to speak and write clearly in one's native language. How much progress has been made since the 1983 publication of *A Nation at Risk?* The National Commission on Excellence in Education found that

Twenty-three million Americans are functionally illiterate by the simplest test of everyday reading, writing, and comprehension.

About 13 percent of all 17-year-olds in the United States can be considered functionally illiterate. Functional illiteracy among minority youth may run as high as 40 percent.

Many 17-year-olds do not possess the "higher-order" intellectual skills we should expect of them. Nearly 40 percent cannot draw inferences from written material (and) only one-fifth can write a persuasive essay....

Progress? According to Jonathan Kozol in his 1985 *Illiterate America*, twenty-five million Americans cannot read above the fourth-grade level. Another thirty-five million can't read above ninth-grade level. That's sixty million people, or approximately 35 percent of the adult population, who can't read the instructions on the front gate of the Information Age. And the problem is not confined to northeast Chicago or the Mississippi swamp. At MIT (no backwater junior college, that) incoming freshmen are subjected to a test of basic writing skills to determine whether they should take the one remedial class offered by the university. Of the 1031 students in the 1984 freshman class, 800, or almost 80 percent, failed the test.

Reading and writing are far more fundamental than computer literacy, for if Johnny — bedraggled effigy of national illiteracy — if Johnny can't read, how will he log on? How will he read software documentation that is already so poorly written as to be incomprehensible to any but inside trackers and psychics? Reading is everything, computer literacy is only something, and their relative importance differs by orders of magnitude. To allow paranoia about computer illiteracy to continue to eclipse efforts to promote the original, the true, literacy is to shortchange our children in the worst way.

Even the term is hype, a case of evocative labeling typical of causes being championed. To put computer literacy, by name-association, on a par with reading and writing is to give it a significance that is not justified, for it is not an extension of what has heretofore been understood as literacy. "The device," insists Charles Suhor, deputy executive director of the National Council of Teachers of English, "is raw propaganda, and does no service to reading and writing (which must now, it seems, be redundantly called 'print literacy')." Of course children should have opportunities to learn about computers as they wish, but not at the expense of this highest priority skill.

Culture

An acquaintance with the basic ideas of the culture — history, literature, music, and art — as well as math and science, observes Weizenbaum, is the foundation of the sense of identity. It is the basis for a child's understanding of himself as rooted in a place that is rich in tradition and, at the same time, gives him a toehold on the future.

"Culture is activity of thought," wrote Alfred North White-head, "and receptiveness of beauty and human feeling. Scraps of information have nothing to do with it. A merely well-informed man is the most useless bore on God's earth." It is critical that children are taught the full constellation of ideas, for it is in the cross-referencing — history of science, for example, understood in relation to other histories — that knowledge begins to sparkle and resonate. It is here that understanding of one subject illuminates understanding of another, and the child begins to take on the breadth of an educated human being.

The arts, the humanities, math, and science — the core subjects in the school curriculum — are being crowded by new classes in technology and by aggressively technology-based teaching techniques. Something has to give, for schools have limited resources and only so much time in the day. As always, it is a question of priorities. Meanwhile, according to the National Commission,

> Only one-third (of all 17-year-olds) can solve a mathematics problem requiring several steps.

> Severe shortages of certain kinds of teachers exist: in the fields of mathematics, science, and foreign languages; and among specialists in education for gifted and talented, language minority, and handicapped students.

> Half of the newly employed mathematics, science, and English
> teachers are not qualified to teach these subjects; fewer than
> one-third of U.S. high schools offer physics taught by qualified
> teachers.

Meanwhile, the schools are teaching (when they succeed in
teaching anything) a few facts, and those often along increasingly specialized paths on the way to employment. The culture
suffers from neglect. Barzun makes the point that, through
specialization, culture ceases to be the property of whomever
wants to enjoy it. Art and the humanities, chopped up into little
morsels and delegated to the experts, become not good things
for the head and heart but goods to be marketed. We are not
giving our children a sufficiently broad sense of the culture for
them either to appreciate its interlocking quality or to keep it
whole.

Social Skills

The arts of negotiation, collaboration, cooperation; the capacity
to imagine the viewpoints of others; the sense that one can
actively shape one's environment, and an appreciation of the
possible consequences of those actions are all aspects of social
skills. One needs only to look at the evening news to find signs
of deficiency in these critical skills. Negotiation is the rarefied
practice of a select few State Department officials and specially
trained units of urban police. As for the rest of us, it seems to
be assumed that we'll learn how to coexist on the fly — at the
dinner table, in the playground, at costly group-therapy week-
ends, and through the women's magazines we read in the grocery check-out line.

Teaching is nurturing a child. It includes not only measured
doses of the facts but the subtle, immeasurable process of enabling a child to learn — to learn reading, writing, art and the
humanities, and the tough-tender skills of human interaction.
It includes not only a dispensing of information but training in
its constructive use. Few are willing to pay for this aspect of
education. It's not one of the basics we're getting back to. In-

stead, education is valued in terms of hours meted out and learning objectives achieved. You can almost buy it by the pound.

Thank God, Our Dogs Are Finally Getting Enough Cheese!

None of what should be our highest priorities are getting much more than lip service in the shadow of computer technology. They pale in relation to a medium that seems so much more attractive, so very sexy and consumable. At once the creation and the leading standard bearer of sci-tech culture, the computer is providing a focus for our related needs to consume and to be a part of something. (Could it be that there is also a certain pleasure in excluding those prophesied technopeasants who don't or can't have the technology?) Like the good consumer product that it is, the computer takes on its own momentum, sniffing out market niches to fill and filling them.

This technology in search of application — a solution, grumbles Weizenbaum, in search of a problem — has found its niche in the educational realm once considered rather sacred. If one is concerned about the quality of education, it now takes stern stuff to resist the conclusion that 1) educational computing is the answer, and 2) the real question is which software and hardware to buy. Welcoming out of well-conditioned habit the latest, brightest product to appear on the shelf, we turn it over in our eager hands, comparing the advertised claims for the new thing with the thing that came out last week, pondering chrome versus anodized black and tacitly allowing the invention of false needs as ridiculous as cheese-flavored dog food.

We get so caught up in today's inventions — CD ROM with 50MB memory, the Amiga 32-bit color machine, or whatever — that we forget we haven't yet figured out how to use yesterday's hardware to the full. The overwhelming majority of good educational software to come out in the next few years could probably be developed on an 8K, no-frills computer from Radio Shack. But it won't be, because we're still too enamored. We're also too busy to pause long enough to wonder whether it makes sense to use the technology as if it were an indispensible vehicle for instruction or to devote relatively huge chunks of time and money to teaching our children how it works.

Consider what happened recently in a third-grade class in a private school in Cambridge, Massachusetts, a school distinguished by an unusual lack of computer hysteria and a corollary appreciation for the multidimensionality of teaching. The kids were having a wonderful time with some cheap wooden "geoboards," getting more by all accounts out of these 49-cent gizmos than they had been from LOGO. Although the teacher could acknowledge that the geoboards were not only cheaper by a factor of several thousand and comparably easier to use, it was very difficult for him to admit that the kids might not need computers. He was embarrassed by the proposition, transfigured by the notion that he *ought* to support computers — even in the face of overwhelming evidence that something else might work at least as well, and in the absence of any but ambivalent evidence of direct, generalizable gains.

It is difficult for any of us to resist the claims made for educational software — claims which follow close upon the heels of needs and problems that didn't seem so pressing before the cure. Hat in hand, the software buyer goes forth under siege by advertisers' claims that their software and their's alone has all the features her children need. A couple of the most commonly claimed benefits are the teaching of "directions" and "problem solving." Many educational software packages for younger kids cite one or both among their list of skills taught. There they are on the package in large print, a black dot beside each skill and a panel of educational experts behind every word. It seems convincing enough. But wait! Couldn't it be true that Pac-Man also teaches directions and problem solving? Since one has to learn both to play the game, Pac-Man could be said to encourage dexterity in these areas. But those claims aren't made for the game because it's neither designed nor packaged as educational. Pac-Man is entertainment, and that's all it needs in order to sell.

Not so for educational software. It must be shown (or at least alleged) to have merit, and merit along certain recognized indices. But the differences between educational and recreational software are often only as deep as the advertising. While the

terms may give the impression of solidity, most educational
claims are so fluffy they could just as well be applied to sneakers.
Imagine the advertisement:

- *Problem Solving* With a pair of new TreadMills on his
  feet, your child will learn to get out of problem situations in a jiffy. "Puzzlers" such as Playing Frisbee on
  Asphalt challenge kids to find creative solutions.

- *Strategy* TreadMills free your child from the drudgery
  of walking, enabling him to turn his attention to more
  advanced skills and concepts such as — How to get from
  there to there in the rain? What about fences? And
  many more.

- *Mapping Skills* Your child is nowhere without Tread-
  Mills. With them, he'll be more than somewhere — he'll
  be able to get somewhere else! An important skill for
  kids of all ages.

- *Teaches 'Over' and 'Under'* TreadMills teach this practical
  skill through real-life applications. The rubber part goes
  under your child's foot, and the laces go over. Only with
  TreadMills — designed to let your child put his best
  foot forward.

- *Critical Learning Skills* Let's face it. The kids of today
  simply aren't critical enough. With TreadMills, they'll
  keep themselves — and everyone around them — on
  their toes.

In a recent radio advertisement, one leading hardware and
business software company had the wit to parody their own
efforts along these lines. Would that their educational counterparts were so droll. Or so honest.

> Recently a man returned from his local computer store having
> purchased the Epson Personal Computer and savoring a $600
> savings on the Epson Executive Tool Kit — a collection of top-
> name business software...specially enhanced to make the most
> of Epson's state-of-the-art simplicity. Well, these powerful pro-
> grams, operating on Epson's uniquely English push button
> keyboard, enabled him to get down to business right away.
> Productivity soared, the man prospered. His children became
> "A" students, his wife dropped fifteen pounds, and the family

beagle, spayed ten years ago, gave birth to a single golden
retriever puppy...,

The computer simultaneously inflates the perceived value of
the instruction to which it is attached and obscures what might
be more important lessons or higher quality learning experiences. The claim that a program teaches certain "educational"
skills takes on an air of credibility it wouldn't have without
computers. The implication is that Mom or Dad or Teacher
should care about those skills as they never have before, and
further, that she or he should look to the computer to teach
them. Some claims are so general they don't say anything of
real importance about the program. Others such as "problem
solving" and "shape recognition" promise things that children
get anyway. (It's like an educational Meadow in a Can — included in this package is a diskette, a 36-page manual, and the
use of the great outdoors!) Puffy claims function as decoys to
attract an eager and therefore somewhat indiscriminate audience. The attraction is strong but insubstantial, since it does not
arise from a match between real needs and useful products.
Consequently, the ever-capricious, over-solicited audience may
turn its back on the product as swiftly as it scooped it up. Said
one elementary school computer-educator in the spring of 1985,
barely six months after problem solving had seemed the greatest
thing since sliced bread, "Problem solving software? Oh, we
don't use that any more." Her school has moved on to something
else.

Amidst the flurry, we forget that children have been taught
shape recognition and the like for eons. The perennial matching
games (letters, numbers, colors) and games involving square
pegs in square holes fall within the shape recognition category.
Virtually every school lesson includes some training in problem-
solving and learning skills. Before computers came along, these
lessons were sometimes so named, sometimes not, but the skills
were always there. If someone had announced ten years ago
that there was soon to be a device to teach shape recognition at
a cost of only half a billion dollars, would we have bought it?
Should we buy it today? The question is anathema since con-
sumerism has taken such firm hold in education. The "how"
takes precedence over the "why." We wonder how to exploit

software for educational purposes before bothering to ask whether it makes sense to do so. By allowing the course of education to be shaped by advertisers' wiles we are falling into the trap set by our own inappropriate expectations.

Should We or Shouldn't We?

Forget the LOGO noise for a moment, and Apple versus IBM; forget about problem solving and shape recognition and K through 12 software curricula. The quiet alternative to viewing the computer as the cutting edge of an inexorable technological movement to which we must respond involves turning the problem on its head. Let us try resequencing the questions, asking first, Do we want or need to utilize the computer in the service of our authentic educational needs? And then — only if the answer is yes — How should we take advantage of the technology? If and only if we decide to teach with and/or about computers, we should do it with both eyes open, both feet on the ground, and at least one hand on the pursestrings.

Does it make sense to use the computer in the service of education? Obviously, it can do a lot of swell things, although like any tool it can do some things better than others. A screwdriver, designed to turn screws, can be used to clean the mud off your shoes, to pry the lid off a paint can, to pick, twist, pound, scrape, and dig. It can be used to puncture a can of V-8 juice, but a churchkey might be more effective. A computer can integrate graphics, text, and sound, but in many cases a book might do a better job of getting the point across. Poor resolution, screenglare, unimaginitive graphics, and eye-boggling typefaces combine to make readability something less than one of the computer's strong points. A computer can be used as a writing instrument, along the lines of Papert's computer-as-pencil vision, but a real pencil or a piece of chalk might be just as good.

It's an indefatigable spoon-feeder, a master at information management, and a servant of self-paced instruction. Should we therefore use it to teach? Not unless it can be made to help teachers do their job, and unless the software content is in keeping with subjects they already teach. Should we teach computer technology as a separate subject because of its pervasiveness in the modern world? Maybe, maybe not. These decisions shouldn't be made arbitrarily, on the basis of availability or convincing advertisements, but in relation to a host of other factors. A science teacher might put plants under a sun lamp to demonstrate the process of photosynthesis. Should sun lamps be used to teach science? By all means, if they can be useful in the hands of a skillful teacher. If the real thing — in this case, sunlight on a manageable schedule — is unavailable or for some other reason inappropriate to the task. And if it makes sense in relation to other educational priorities.

If we do choose to devote one hour of every child's day to educational computing, what other subject will be left without a chair when the music stops? Will it be history? Will it be art? Must we convert our schools to high-tech training centers, or are there better things to do with those resources?

Most current approaches to educational computing are inappropriate either in terms of the medium or real school needs and budgets. Mainstream CAI fails to exploit the tremendous power of the medium. It's like taking a helicopter to the grocery store. On the other end of the spectrum are the would-be schools of the future, those oases in the educational desert that are irrigated by corporate and university funds and world-class technological expertise. Experimentation of this type is to be applauded, but it must be seen as experimentation, not the creation of replicable models.

Recognized for its power, educational computing must also be understood as profoundly weak. It is ridiculous to think that the computer can replace the thoughtful sensitivity of a teacher, for it can barely teach states and capitols and that only with a helping hand. It cannot replace the printed or spoken word, only support it with visual anecdote. It is said to be inherently interactive, but that depends on the software, and the software — egad! — is almost uniformly terrible.

It is also ridiculous to assume that computing should be available to every child, as if it has some inherent property that could benefit all children across the board. It doesn't. Furthermore, such assumptions place an unfair and unrealistic burden on what is little more than a fledgling artform. There is someone in every crowd, for example, who clamors for special needs software in a tone reflecting a combination of hurt and a sense of entitlement. These people seem to think that everyone else is getting software, and that all the designers have to do is shift the template seven degrees to the left to produce software for special needs. Their attitude springs from a view of software verging on the mystical, as if the culture had conjured up educational software to solve the problems of education. Software has no such destiny or obligation. It did not burst upon the scene, fully formed and charged with teaching responsibilities. The medium was painstakingly developed, after centuries of research, for the purpose of waging precise war, and what we have in education are the leavings and the spin-offs. We're doing pretty well at making the best of it, but the stuff is no panacea.

Software is just something that happens to be here now. In educational terms, it's an accident, a windfall. It should neither be dismissed or venerated, but used as one of a tremendous collection of tools to help children learn in all the ways they do learn. In solitude and with peers, parents, and teachers. On and off the computer. At home and in school and in between. Let us consider the computer as just one, somewhat flawed device to help the teacher stage intriguing environments which leave plenty of room for teaching, as the vehicle for an in-the-classroom field trip to somewhere else, as an alternative to TV. These are worthy goals, albeit modest. Despite tremendous pressure to make it a revolution, let us think of educational technology as an experimental artform, something small and possibly wonderful.

Lap Learning

The computer can do very little for us in support of the first two priority items, literacy and knowledge of the culture. However, it can be instrumental, in perhaps surprising ways, in teaching social skills and enhancing the social aspects of learning. Teachers polled in the Johns Hopkins survey said the greatest impact of the computer has been social, far more than on achievement per se. They noted that students were more enthused about schooling, more inclined to help one another and to work without provocation from the teacher. This is not a function of superficial motivation, but something deeper. Although the computer is often cited as a motivator, there is no real evidence to support this claim. Charles Suhor contends that the

> evidence of children's "natural" enchantment with computer programming is largely anecdotal and certainly hyperbolic. I have heard such stories mainly about children of MIT professors, and from parents who recently sank several thousand dollars into personal computers and a truckload of peripherals and software.

Indeed, it seems that whatever initial interest the computer may have held, at school or the arcade it is waning. Computer class is becoming just another class. But there remains the possibility that the computer can sponsor healthy social interactions between people of all ages.

There are arguments in favor and against exposure of young children to computers. Both sides concern themselves with the impact, good or bad, of various kinds of software on tender minds while ignoring the relationship fostered between parent and child by joint computer activity. Let's keep our facts straight. What little kids probably love most about software isn't the software at all but the chance to sit on Dad's or Mom's lap. Once they're snugly in place on the parental lap, kids love whatever is going on. Their parent's excitement about the computer is contagious. Another possibility is that parents are so enchanted with their new toy, the only way for the kid to do some lapsitting is to hang around the computer. They get to like it after a while.

Listen to parents and teachers talk about their experiences with little kids and computers. At least three-quarters of the anecdotes one hears have Mom or Dad or some fond adult playing a key role. Kids also seem to grasp concepts more quickly and with better retention when a parent is closely involved in the learning process. "Scaffolding" is how child psychologists describe what the parents are doing by providing support to the learning process; the scaffold is gradually withdrawn as the child gains competence. Let's call what the kids are doing "lap learning."

What kind of software is useful with little kids who can't read yet and can't do much with the keyboard? Many preschool software programs are designed such that toddlers can proceed intuitively, once they get started. Other programs come with plastic pieces that fit over the keys, to give kids something bigger to touch. At least one children's program, Muppet Learning Keys, has the keyboard arranged in alphabetical order. This is nice, but beside the point.

The limitations with which little kids come to the computer need not be considered limitations at all, but opportunities for lap learning. There are spelling programs and memory games and games with colored squares. Even the simplest of them must be explained by a parent, a teacher, or an older child, and the deeper and more advanced the software, the more someone else has to be involved.

It doesn't matter what the program is about, so long as it is appropriate for kids. Anything that brings an adult and a child together in good fun is infinitely more valuable than software used by a child alone. Parents need not bore themselves with colored trianges, but can start with something sufficiently complex to interest all participants — a flight simulator, for example. Children can enter big worlds if they come in at an appropriate level. What they learn may not be "shape recognition" or "keyboard dexterity" or whatever the package claims to teach. They'll simply have the joy and the compound benefits of being with an adult who cares about them.

Learning Standing Up

If we are to use computers in schools, we should recognize that some of the same issues we face with younger kids apply to children of school age. Chief among them is the fact that environment is infinitely more critical to learning than the specific features of a software program. Anything can be fun or not fun; anything can be a valuable learning experience if it has the appropriate elements. What are the surroundings — are they comfortable or crowded, condusive to learning or distracting? Who are the participants — peers, teachers, or no one but

Freddie and the machine? Are human interactions possible? Are they plentiful, healthy, diverse? Is the atmosphere open or closed, supportive or authoritarian, interventionist or solitary? These are the questions we ought to be asking.

As with preschool computing, the limitations of the kids, the environment and the technology are all opportunities for learning. The fact that not all thirty kids in a class can see a single $6\frac{1}{2}'' \times 9\frac{1}{2}''$ screen need not be cause for despair or hasty turning to yet another technological remedy. In rushing to solve each technological problem, we rob ourselves of having to figure out how to make the technology work naturally in the classroom. The eight-foot screen, for example, which magnifies the smaller screen for all the class to see, may solve some of the delivery problems. But in doing so it may also mask certain other, more profound, educational problems such as the educational ineffectiveness of the material. The limitations of the smaller screen fling the teacher back on her own resources. She must continue to teach much as she did before the machine came rolling into her room, and that's just fine.

The school itself is an environment that must be dealt with, new technology aside. As appalling in some cases as that environment may have become, destructive to the spirit, dealer of death at an early age, it has certain features we can turn to advantage and certain roles too important to be abandoned. School is a social organization, jammed to the rafters with thirty or so kids per class, who haven't come to school nearly so much to learn states and capitols as to find out how their friends are. School is crucial to the transformation of children into socialized, appropriately trained adults. It also serves as a custodian while we work, and provides some compensatory attention such as baseline medical care and second-language education. A 1978 Rand Corporation study found that many of the innovative programs of the sixties failed to take hold largely due to a failure to conceive of schools as complex social systems. We must learn from that experience, or waste another decade.

Futuristic visions of solitary, computer-aided learning continue to ignore the twin facts that people need people, and that schools exist already as throbbing people-to-people institutions. Separated by technology or any other divisive tool, students break out of cloistered cells to be together. Allowing students to work on (or off) the computer in small groups often produces greater results, for in those groups students challenge and encourage each other. They give one another feedback far more meaningful and intense than could ever be provided by a computer. Such interaction also helps break the shell of compulsive programmers who control the machine because they cannot control anything else. Of course children need a chance to work alone, to sharpen their skills before they bring them into the sometimes harsh arena of the group. But working with the group once they've become skillful gives them the thrilling, reinforcing opportunity to show off, and share, their mastery. It helps them learn, and learn to be human.

The Land of Aha's

Derek Bok suggests that technology's greatest benefit is not in yielding direct instructional gains but in obliging us to think more clearly about the process of learning and teaching. Its catalytic effect will surely result in improved software quality in the various modes — computer-aided instruction, tool programs, simulations, and games. We'll review each of those modes in the following chapters. In the meantime, let's stay with the social idea. The surprising social impact of computers hints at new ways to integrate formal and informal learning and new ways to understand motivation.

Consider that adults generally learn with a purpose in mind — to do a job, fix a car, prepare *Escalopes de Veau Chasseur*. The skills and concepts they acquire make them better at an activity that is important to them. School children, in contrast, are taught abstract information without their knowing the purpose this knowledge might serve aside from meeting the demands of the curriculum. Their relatively limited frame of reference renders them not well prepared to learn for arbitrary reasons, yet they are obliged to do so every day by a system designed to teach skills and concepts for which the rationale is invisible or, at best, said to become clear "when you're older." Since they have no viable alternative but to comply — they know, as James Herndon noted in *How to Survive in Your Native Land*, that the only choice is between school or jail — they learn math, social studies, spelling and all the rest for no reason other than that they're told to. If asked, "Why are you memorizing Presidents' names (or searching for the value of $x + 4 - xy$)?", they will repeat the litany: "Because it's good for me (and because it will show up on a test at the end of the week)." Without a sense of their possible utility and no context to attach them to, it is hard to remember, harder still to understand, these vacuum-packed abstractions.

Purely contextual learning is likewise limited. A child who knows baseball, for example, may become quite facile at averaging and other baseball-based skills, but in the absence of a framework with broader application, he may not be able to transfer those skills to settings outside the playing field. Neither abstract nor contextual learning alone is sufficient. A 1984 report for the National Academy of Sciences, "Research Briefing on Information Technology in Precollege Education," asserts

> Cognitive research confirms that knowledge learned without conceptual understanding or functional application to problems is either forgotten or remains inert when it is needed in situations that differ from ones in which the knowledge was acquired.

It is doubtless important that children learn the skills and concepts prescribed by the curriculum. The pity is that they often have to wait a long time for the moment they can apply their knowledge to an activity that is meaningful to them and more compelling than a Friday afternoon spot quiz. When that moment at last occurs, they have an Aha! experience. "Aha!" they exclaim, "I remember learning that in school," or "Aha! That must be what Mrs. Potter was talking about!"

The Land of Aha's is thus that fertile valley between contextual vacationlands and the mountainous abstract, that enlightened place where Mrs. Potter's teachings, stored without reference among obligatory piles of facts, begin to come together in sensible form and where things learned in the playground get connected to other things learned in the classroom. It is a place rarely visited within the bounds of school. Even less is it acknowledged as a valuable locus for learning, for school is the site of "formal education," the supposed polar opposite of informal education, and nothing in between has an official name. Formal education is set apart from everyday life and society; there is *school* and there is *not-school*. School is hierarchical, with the teacher responsible for imparting knowledge and skill, and it is based on an explicit pedagogy and curriculum. Informal education, in contrast, is imbedded in daily life. It is personal, interactive, reciprocal — with the learning (inexplicit) being a function of observation and experimentation. Motivation is intrinsic to the process.

Watch the Birdie

Our culture's insistence on a sharp distinction between formal and informal education has isolated school children from one another and from the grounding which makes learning make sense. It has also estranged the "formal" learning process from the desire to learn. The study of language is too detached from natural communication, the study of art from what we feel is beautiful, the study of science from our wonder at the world. Driven by what we take as technology's promise to teach and yes, to motivate, we have set our children up to learn facts and figures from that omniscient, anonymous machine and/or how to steer the thing around the parking lot by way of BASIC programming. We have seen fit to make explicit each and every one of our educational goals, dismissing as unimportant the hard-to-measure, shrugging off intrinsic value — and intrinsic motivation — in favor of a system of explicit objectives paired with extrinsic rewards. We have cut formal education free from its roots, trading meaning for definition, and sanitizing what had been a rather sweaty process in exchange for a squeaky-clean set of goals and achievements that have little to do with learning.

Certainly we want our children to learn. Moreover we want them to become learners — individuals willing, indeed, eager to formulate questions, seek out answers, and share their understanding with others. We strive through schooling to launch them as autonomous learners who do this for the joy, the satisfaction, and the life-necessity of it, quite apart from the meager rewards and punishments of the classroom. Our methods have backfired in part because of those very rewards and punishments. By trying to be excruciatingly clear about what a kid is supposed to learn (presumably as much for his benefit as for the administration's) we have made him self-conscious, as in having his picture taken. By injecting the system with spurious rewards designed to induce kids to learn what we assume, perhaps erroneously, they would otherwise find uninteresting, we may inhibit their natural desire to participate in educational activities.

A series of intriguing field experiments by psychologists Mark Lepper, David Greene, and Richard Nisbett, reported in the *Journal of Personality and Social Psychology*, explored the effects of extrinsic rewards and what is called "adult surveillance" on children's intrinsic motivation. The methodologies varied, the studies were short-term, and the results were somewhat contradictory, but there were a few consistent findings. Children who had undertaken an activity expecting an extrinsic reward — a prize, a treat unrelated to the activity but contingent on participation — worked more quickly during the experimental sessions. But in subsequent sessions, when the reward was no longer expected, their interest dropped below their own initial level as well as that of control group participants who had not expected a reward from the start. This decrease in interest was especially pronounced when the activity was itself entertaining or stimulating. Long-term maintenance of behavior — sustained interest, in other words, one of the cornerstones of autonomous learning — was found to be problematic when repeated pairings of an extrinsic reinforcer with a task led to a view of task and reward as inherently inseparable. "Why should I?" asks the child who has been trained to study, to mow the lawn, even to play a game for arbitrary reasons unrelated, except by forced association, to the activity. It's like the "sugar blues" or a caffeine low, when one's energy plummets lower than it was before the 3 PM Snickers Bar or the fourth cup of coffee. By chronically motivating school children by such false measures, we risk losing not only their momentary attention but their hearts.

Children in the studies who had been placed under surveillance also showed less subsequent interest than those not previously monitored. Simply knowing that one's performance is being observed and evaluated by someone else, even when no tangible reward is expected, appears to be enough to squash one's interest. It also blocks the free-flowing interchange so natural in the playground. When teachers supervise play, the range of opportunities for children to initiate, discuss, and change the rules is narrowed significantly.

Surveillance has as another side-effect, an ugly attributional cycle revealed in L. H. Strickland's classic study of workers and their supervisors. The supervisor comes to distrust the motivations of those under his watchful eye, regarding them as driven primarily by the surveillance itself — hence less internally motivated, hence less trustworthy, hence less likely to perform satisfactorily in the absence of surveillance. The subordinate (read *student*) likewise is undermined. To the extent he sees himself engaging in an activity under strong extrinsic pressure, he attributes his own behavior to those pressures. He comes to see himself as lacking any intrinsic interest in the activity or any intrinsic motivation to perform well.

If we wish our children to become autonomous learners, we should note that any system that increases their dependence on artificial contingencies existing only within the system detracts from the goal. This applies directly to educational computing. The contingencies built into software programs tend to be exaggerated, whether they're the often inappropriate graphic "rewards" that too many CAI programs offer — explosions, dancing chickens, and so forth — or the formal "good job" of the electronic supervisor. To the extent that these prompts are out of proportion, they may be detrimental to the learning process they're supposed to enhance. Not that extrinsic rewards, in or out of educational software, should be abandoned altogether. Not that we should turn the kids loose without any supervision. But if we wish to foster interest in learning that stays alive without prompting, we should prompt only as much as is absolutely necessary. What reinforcers we do use should be natural and as salient to the task as possible.

In the Land of Aha's, learning is prompted by a blend of gentle extrinsic reinforcers and the motivations inherent in the learning situation. Objectives are imbedded in activity. The gap between learning and doing is closed in recognition of the fact that formal and informal education are not polar opposites but mingling points along a spectrum. No one mode of teaching is sufficient, certainly no one style of computerized education — not CAI, not programming, not games and simulations alone. Computers can help, but they alone are insufficient to teach or motivate. We need a variety of teaching methods as diverse as children's learning styles and the subjects to be taught, an amalgam of methods supporting the teaching of hard-boiled data and the squishy subjects, of history and literature, science, math, reading and writing, and the social skills. A game may not be the best way to teach *The House of Seven Gables* any more than CAI should be trusted as the single vehicle for teaching states and capitols. Whatever collection of methods are employed, their combined effect should be the promotion of active learning independent of phony contingencies and grounded in reality through the kind of experience that gives information meaning and value.

The Yellow Brick Road

If computers are important to school-based education — and it does seem that they can make a useful contribution — then it must also be important that we use them well. They must be handled by people who understand teaching, with and without computers. It doesn't matter what the subject is or even, necessarily, what kind of software is being used. The teacher is by far the most important element in an effective learning situation. "A discussion of teaching aids," wrote Jerome Bruner in *The Process of Education*, "may seem like an unusual context in which to consider a teacher's role in teaching. Yet, withal, the teacher constitutes the principle aid in the teaching process."

Teachers are under tremendous pressure, as we've seen — pressure to use computers and to get results. As budgets are cut and schools close, overcrowding the schools which stay open, teachers are obliged simultaneously to be subject matter experts, methodological wizards, psychologists, technologists, and managers of bulging thirty-kid classrooms. The computer as a replacement for these teachers cannot come close to fulfilling the role. Indeed, computers will not automate or streamline the teaching job, or make it any easier. If anything, they will make it harder.

Most teachers are nonetheless excited by the possibilities of working with computers in the classroom and are willing, up to a point, to risk rethinking old patterns to embrace the new technology. It has even been suggested that the real revolution is in teaching, and that the teachers are changing more than the kids. Fifth-grade teachers are having third graders teach LOGO. Other adventurous types have turned their classrooms into technologically-enhanced three-ring circuses. And all this due, presumably, to the provocative influence of the computer.

These changes are all well and good, but we risk being glib about the impact of computers on teaching. Suppose someone were to walk up to a teacher, all smiles, as if announcing a big prize, and say, "You're in luck! There's a revolution coming on and because of it, you're going to teach in a whole new way." That teacher would probably say, "Get lost! And don't come back until you have something that will help me teach the way I do now." Teachers, like all adults, are creatures of habit, and although they have been commendably open to the new technology, they're not really going to change *how* they teach, any more than they would how they walk or drive a car, not unless it's proven that the new tools and methods of educational computing will make what they do a little easier or better.

So let's not get too fired up about changing classroom teaching styles, as if the introduction of computers obliged us to throw out the old methods and bring in the new, whatever they might be. It's a lousy goal and a dangerous fantasy, and no teacher should be expected to subscribe. Change would be happening more slowly if there weren't so much hype and hysteria about shovelling computers into the schools. It would be more appropriate if we slowed ourselves way down. If we granted teachers time, lots of time, to assimilate the new technology. And if the software we designed were as close as possible to the way teachers teach right now, which is admirable and about a thousand times better than what they're given credit for.

Teachers who currently use computers have added this complication to an already complicated job. (Others have learned enough to conclude that they don't need to use computers, thanks anyway.) They have to learn how to run the thing, a task sometimes so onerous as to crush even terrific enthusiasm. They have to figure out how to integrate the machine into the classroom, a project blessed with much good advice — all of it contradictory and little of it directly applicable to their unique situation. They have to choose software, likewise a nightmare. They have to teach their students how to use it, although the students often know more about computers than the teacher, in which case he or she has to deal with that potentially humiliating knowledge discrepancy. Once they have the computer up and running, teachers immediately have to contend with a host of new classroom management problems as well as new challenges in teaching.

All this and more, yet teachers are not getting adequately trained. They're getting one-shot, one-day workshops conducted by computer company representatives who know nothing about education or instructional methods. This is user training, not teacher training at all. Sometimes they just get canned instruction — a little introductory lesson on floppy disk, sometimes no instruction at all. The teacher who is fortunate or resourceful enough to gain some sophistication in matters technological is more than likely to seek greener, higher-paying pastures in industry.

Poor and/or inadequate teacher training is not a good way to launch a revolution, even a modest little micro-transformation, in the way kids are taught. The human side of the enterprise is ignored with predictable results. Poorly trained teachers are unlikely to take full or appropriate advantage of computers despite what may be the best of intentions. They may become frustrated, anxious, and bitter about ever-increasing demands and administrative insensitivity. The kids may remain uninvolved with computers in any significant way, and the school district would be out a bundle.

The problem with teacher training is that we don't know what to train them in, any more than we know how to use the machines with kids. Do we train teachers to use the computer as an instructional medium, as a tool or tool-making tool, as a modeling device, or as something else altogether? One important lesson for teachers and students alike is that the creators of computer programs are every bit as fallible as the authors of textbooks. Teachers must be taught to "computer-proof" their students, encouraging them to verify everything they gather from the screen against common sense and other reliable sources. Nothing else about teacher training is certain.

The next fifteen to twenty years should be a period of intense exploration and experimentation, not one of premature commitment to wrap-around software or any other stock format for the use of computers in schools. With rigidly defined curriculum goals, often accompanied by a prescription for achieving them, there is currently little room for creative endeavor. Rewards and incentives for teachers are skewed in such a way as to discourage risk taking and innovation. If the next two decades are to yield innovative applications appropriate to real teaching needs, then teachers must be encouraged to take chances. The focus of change and integration will be teachers who can combine their pedagogical wisdom with a growing intimacy with computer technology. These teachers do not need to become computer experts, but they do need a thorough understanding of the capabilities and limitations of the computer. Its possible uses, bounded only by the imagination and resources of the user, will follow the distinct styles of individual teachers.

The next fifteen to twenty years should in fact be just the beginning of an endless "mess-around" period. Things are happening so fast these days that answers seem to be just around the corner. Urged to experiment with computers, people think in terms of weeks or months, imagining that the messy phase will last until January, March at the latest. We should make it last for the next twenty decades! For there are no answers, just questions and priorities and a small collection of new tricks to help children learn.

5.

The Indefatigable Drillmaster

Computer: *Who was the first president of the United States?*
1. *Thomas Jefferson*
2. *George Washington*
3. *Abraham Lincoln*

Student: Abraham Lincoln

Computer: *Sorry. Abraham Lincoln was president of the United States during the Civil War from 1861 to 1865. The first president served from 1789 to 1797 and had previously been commander-in-chief of the Continental Army during the American Revolution. Would you like to try again?*

Student: George Washington

Computer: *Good work.*

This is typical CAI fare, a question-and-answer-format (yes/no or multiple choice) with feedback. It may include brief explanations, graphics, sound, a summary. It may be dry and dull or bright and playful. It may be disguised as a game, offering inducements more intense than receipt of a printed pat on the head, particularly if it is aimed at younger children. "Alligators Prompt Correct Answers" is the pitch for an English usage tutorial for grades 3 through 6. If you answer correctly, you move up the steps of a pyramid, away from a pit of writhing, snapping alligators. If you get the wrong answer, you move down. The object of a program called Missile Math is "to position the gun over the correct answer and launch a missile so that it destroys an enemy spaceship as it traverses the screen."

The hope of computer-aided instruction is to employ the computer in the service of instruction as if it were a highly adept teacher, an expert who, unlike most human experts, is graced by infinite patience and wisdom about the sequence in which that expertise should be conveyed. The computer is expected to make this exquisite service available to millions of children, each of whom, wrote computer education pioneer Patrick Suppes, "will have access to what Philip of Macedon's son Alexander enjoyed as a royal prerogative: the personal services of a tutor as well-informed and responsive as Aristotle." CAI is a leveller, like cars and television, a design in keeping with the democratic ideals of public education. To the average class of twenty-five students — five of whom are on the ball, fifteen are sort of there in the bulging middle, and five don't even know the question — CAI offers something for everyone.

With its individualized, self-paced instruction, CAI is touted as an effective solution to the problem of school teachers having to target their efforts to the middle of the class, letting the brightest children drift in fallow boredom and the slower kids wander deeper into ignorance. With CAI, it is said, every child has a tutor. Every child does the problems: he must respond, cannot be passive as in a lecture situation. Every child can take his or her sweet time, whatever it takes to master the material regardless of the pace of other students. If it takes him less time to complete a lesson than the majority of the class, fine! He can move on to more advanced studies. If it takes longer, no problem; the machine is patient. If he needs more than class time to study the lesson, or was absent and needs to catch up, he can turn to the computer after class (or at home) to practice, practice, practice until it's perfect. The best CAI will aid this final step by pointing out where the problem areas lie and to what further study the student might turn to correct the deficiency.

e. e. cummings Returns

One of the reasons for CAI's popularity, or at least for its widespread use, is the seeming ease with which it can be designed. This is an illusion shared by many teachers and others inclined to design the stuff themselves, and to a lesser but more dangerous extent by commercial producers. CAI's linear, step-by-step format is consistent with both the most pedestrian teaching methods and the most rudimentary forms of programming. As a result, design and implementation are joined by a kind of circular logic in which CAI becomes the standard application for which computer systems are designed and thence the most readily created product of those systems.

What is happening among do-it-yourselfers is reminiscent of the early sixties, when college students became poets overnight by dropping the upper case. "it's easy," they said. "if e. e. cummings can do it, so can i." Too many educational software developers are dropping the upper case in their programs, especially CAI. The technology is accessible, and the skills seem easy to come by. All you need is a microcomputer in the diningroom — no machine tools, no toxic fumes, no boss. The labor issues are equalized: you do all the work.

A recent article in *COMPUTE!* entitled "Programming the TI: Writing an Educational Program" begins: "I'm sure you already know or have read what a 'good' educational program should contain." The problem is put forward: "The hardest part...is deciding the topic and the type of program — drill and practice, tutorial, simulation, game, etc." And then the problem is whisked away: "I picked...the Morse code, and decided to do a drill-and-practice program." What follows is a step-by-step explanation of how the writer developed the program, beginning with a decision to use the ampersand and percent sign to represent dashes and dots in the program (easier to type, more accurate) and winding up with suggested quiz variations. The program, in BASIC, is printed in full, so one can type it. Alternatively, one can obtain a copy by sending $3 and a blank diskette to a mailing address in Utah.

There once was a widespread belief that teachers would be the greatest source of educational software, and despite the lack of supporting evidence, vestiges of this myth linger on. It is true that with some programming experience, or with the more palatable help of authoring languages (CAI-generating CAI), teachers can create their own drill-and-practice programs and tutorials. They can tailor programs to suit particular needs, covering subjects not included in the regular curriculum or learning objectives shared by only a small subset of the class, or create new programs which they may be able to sell to a wider audience. Fortunately (or un-, depending on one's views), this effort takes a tremendous amount of time — time which is better spent working with students. It also takes considerable skill in programming and, if one hopes for commercial success, in marketing. These skills may not be worth acquiring relative to others a teacher might develop to better purpose.

The benefit of do-it-yourself software design is more in the process than the product, for the latter is likely to be educationally insubstantial. The process itself, aside from time and money constraints — the effort to create software, to adapt a magazine recipe to one's own machine, to modify the recipe to suit one's needs — is good, clean fun. It is also educational, for the designer is forced to think deeply about how to teach. Regardless of whether the product is used, the educator gains new insights about teaching in the course of designing software to help her teach.

But creating quality programs that transform the computer into an even moderately complex instructional medium turns out to be harder than it might seem, harder, certainly, than early enthusiasts predicted. The designer of a tutorial program, for example, must anticipate most possible answers to each question in order to allow for meaningful dialogue. Each question branches in several directions, each with its own new question, which branches in turn to still other new questions. This rat's nest is known as a "combinatorial explosion." The programming task that began so simply becomes almost infinitely complex, exceeding, potentially, the capabilities of both the machine and the programmer.

Even if all responses could be anticipated and the appropriate branches built into the program, true dialogue involves interpretation and shared referencing that is not — and, for a long time to come, will not be — programmable. Bok offers this example:

> One can describe a home run by stating that "the ball sailed over the center-field wall" or "Jim blasted a round-tripper" or "the big first baseman muscled it out of the park." A computer would have to be programmed with more information than most machines can currently handle simply to interpret all the variations that can occur in conversing about most subjects. Worse yet, no one knows how to formulate a set of rules by which a computer can compare statements like these and recognize them as equivalents. A human being with adequate knowledge and experience perceives the similarities instantly. We simply do not know how the process works.

If we *could* program the process, would we want the product? By conversing with a machine that can respond to "Jim blasted a round-tripper," we may satisfy our curiosity and perhaps gain some instruction, but not much, for all the work it takes.

The Sistine Chapel Committee

Anyone can drop their upper case and call it poetry, and almost anyone, with a little effort, can design a modest CAI program or two. The challenge is much greater in the realm of large-scale commercial production, where publishers and their stable of designers set about to develop entire software curricula. The goal, in the grand words of one leading publisher, is "to stimulate, motivate, and educate students from kindergarten through grade twelve," and to do it at a rate fast enough to satisfy customer demand and in a high enough volume to make it worthwhile.

Publishers have a choice. They can attempt to coordinate the efforts of hundreds of independent software firms scattered across the country, each employing half a dozen high-powered software designers. This method would be likely to produce livelier software, but it is too expensive and unwieldy to be either economically or managerially feasible. Or they can do it in-house.

Enter the committee — a host of experts including educational specialists, teachers, evaluators, and a software manager to coordinate the process. The problem here is that group process tends to undervalue the creative effort, producing results, when it produces anything at all, which range from bad to absurd. Imagine the workings of the Sistine Chapel Committee:

> "Hey Mike, would you put some angels in this corner? And make sure they have those blue highlights. The color subcommittee says there's not enough blue."

> "Oh God," mutters Michaelangelo from the scaffolding, getting paint on his teeth.

Now imagine the educational equivalent of the Sistine Chapel Committee. They start with a stack of clearly defined learning objectives consistent with the curriculum goals of the audience. From there, they build a huge web of theory about how kids learn grammar, for example, a theory rich with new and exciting methodologies developed by experts in the field to motivate, stimulate, and help children learn. They stick a few bells and whistles on top of everything, just to perk things up.

> "Does anyone know a game?"

> "We need excitement! The research indicates that excitement is condusive to learning."

> "I know! Let's blow up dangling participles. The kid pulls the pin on the diphthong bomb when the participle dangles in the middle of the screen."

When all this is assembled, they test the cognitive, neurophysiological, syntonic, epistemological, psychomechanical, combinatorial, and motivational effects of the program on a handful of kids, tweak it here and there if necessary, and pack it up for sale.

What is happening to educational software is not unlike what happened to Nancy Drew. The original Nancy Drew books are unarguably flawed in their portrayals of sex roles, racial issues, and work options (although teenage girls could do a lot worse than have Nancy Drew as a role model; she is wonderfully competent and assertive, shockingly so from a distance of fifty years). Early Nancy Drews aren't P. D. James, but they're pretty good, and kids read them. The new and revised Nancy Drews, in contrast, are produced by a publishing syndicate busy purging the classics of stereotypes and squeezing out new books as smooth as Cream of Wheat and as inspiring as the Red Guard Ballet.

Increasingly, educational software is designed by such committees assembled for the purpose of producing widely acceptable software at regular intervals. The committees include all the right ingredients, but rarely are they able to integrate their various contributions into a learning-intense yet enjoyable product. Established in response to an economic imperative to produce quickly and reliably, the group falters in part due to its own bulk. Unwieldy interrelationships make it slow and inefficient. Output is flattened to the lowest common denominator. Textbooks are also produced by committee, with similar results. With CAI, we compound that mistake severalfold by transposing the humdrum content of mass-produced textbooks to the newer and excessively more expensive medium.

Just the Facts

The most common application format for educational software, CAI is also the most disappointing. It is disparaged with good reason by many educators, for it reflects a limited, limiting pedagogy rife, as Henry Olds has observed, with counter-productive hidden messages. It also fails to live up to the promise of being an effective tutor to the masses. We should perhaps have been alerted to its shortcomings by the fact that real teachers do not act like CAI. It seems that they know something CAI designers don't.

CAI deals in facts, those hard little nuggets, and it deals with them in a manner which implies that once one sorts out the true from the false — a distinction unburdened in CAI by doubt or ambiguity — one needs only to assemble the facts into patterns to arrive at reality. CAI poses a series of questions, and students are to answer these and no other, choosing their answers among a limited set provided, as are the questions, by the machine. Students are not asked (who's listening?) to frame their own questions or hypotheses about the material under study. And their answers, CAI implies, are either right or wrong, with nothing in between and nothing of interest in the junk heap called "wrong" save for possible pointers to what is "right." The message hidden underneath the commendations, the scoldings, alligators and guns: learning is in control of an omniscient other — someone or something whose representative is the screen and to whose knowledge and pedagogy the student must submit for the duration of the program, narrowing his intake to discrete, serial facts and his output to "yes" or "no."

There are subjects which lend themselves to computer-aided instruction insofar as they require the rote memorization of terms, procedures, routines, rules, facts. Foreign language vocabulary is a good example, as are the rules of grammar. The rules of accounting, how to use a word processor, the names of the muscles of the back (fifth layer: *Semispinalis dorsi, Semispinalis colli, Multifidus spinae, Rotatores spinae, Supraspinalis,* etc.) — these must be learned by rote and thus are receptive to the CAI treatment.

Most subjects are not so compliant. Thomas Kuhns, in *The Structure of Scientific Revolutions*, reminds us that even science, the model for all that would be hard-edged, must be recognized in the long historical view as the currently accepted paradigm — a set of laws, theories, and applications which has not been accepted from time immemorial and will not, we must assume, be unchallenged in times to come. Aside from dates, battles, and kings, history is a subject whose substance is interpretation. Most "facts" are points of view. "Entire Constitution Explained in Parts," screams the advertisement for a sixth-grade courseware package with all the nerve and nonsense of the *National Inquirer.* Literature is by definition fictional. Its "facts" are metaphorical, its impact as much on the spirit as the brain. ("I'm not interested in fiction because it isn't true," said one of a batch of technology students asked to speculate on what should give way to computer education at the high school level. Another candidate was history "because you can always look it up if you need it.") Sociology and psychology, having gained their legitimacy through adoption of scientific methods, are likewise subjects which must also be studied from qualitative perspectives impossible to squeeze into the CAI format. To so reduce important, open-ended concepts is to trivialize them beyond recognition. The alternative is to omit from the program the social, moral, and interpretive aspects of an issue and thereby contribute to the erosion of respect for whatever resists compartmentalization.

Step-by-Step

With CAI, even sophisticated branching programs, learning is a step-by-step process in which one must suspend creative insights, cognitive leaps, and other nonlinear phenomena. The technology won't allow anything more. But current cognitive research indicates that learning is, to the contrary, a highly intuitive process wherein the learner adapts patterns already in mind to solve new problems.

A child learns to make sense of the world as she acts upon it and succeeds in coordinating her actions with the effects of those actions. Though she may begin with little more than an indistinguishable collection of sensations and a pair of hands, that pair of hands is the cornerstone of what Papert calls a "microworld of pairing" in which Mother/Father, knife/fork, and left sock/right sock have something in common. Development proceeds as these fledgling understandings are tested, revised, broadened, and interrelated in increasingly complex, multidimensional patterns. Information set in a human or anthropomorphic context feeds these patterns more readily than data, which is necessarily abstract, and which seems invariably to settle in a place in the brain which holds information like a sieve. A child shown pictures of a hundred people's faces along with pictures of a hundred houses will remember almost none of the houses, but the faces will come back to him so vividly it's as if he made up instant stories about each one. He can probably tell you what each person was wearing and what they might have had for breakfast. Another child, snuggled in her mother's enveloping arms, listens to a story about a blue-haired frog who alone can save the townspeople locked in a trance by the spell-binding cabbage vendor. Mom reads the story once and then again, the second time changing the frog's hair to pink on page 147. "No!" the child will shout, bolting out of half-sleep, "the frog has *blue* hair!"

When a fact has a place to go, when it fits into a context that makes sense, however fanciful, it will curl up like a child in pajamas and stay a long time. But context is notably absent in today's versions of CAI, or deranged by gratuitous association with guns and alligators. To learn from CAI requires, accordingly, a higher level of motivation than can usually be expected from students asked to learn something of no apparent utility. Contrary to its claims to liberate the teacher, CAI demands that he fill in the gaps, making the connections between new fact and old, fresh insight and deeper understanding. This can be rather awkward, for the software does not acknowledge a need for his help. He has to hover around a machine dispensing software that does not include him in the question-answer loop and thereby interferes with her intuitions about how and when to intervene. Supplementing CAI is like cutting in on someone on the dance floor. What is the teacher to do when he senses a child needs help? Switch off the computer? Stick his head in front of the screen? Rotate the child forty-seven degrees to refocus her attention? It's a dirty job but someone has to do it, for the learning process is at its most inefficient when stripped of the story line and the other nonlinear patterns that help learners make sense of the world. Who will make the connections if we replace teachers with CAI-dispensing machines?

No Learner Is an Island

Learning is inherently interactive, beginning with a question, moving to an exploration, and then on to an expression of what has been learned. Each step is a dialogue, and true dialogue, which requires each participant to interpret the stories, allusions, and shared references of the other, is currently well beyond the capabilities of the machine and even further beyond the capabilities of mainstream CAI programs. Second guessing is what one learns to do with CAI, not intuitive cognitive leaping, not cooperative learning. One learns instead that learning is an isolated activity in which a solitary student engages, one-on-one, with a machine. This is taken as given, and the problems fall from there. Reported *Newsweek* in March 1984, complaining that the computer revolution in education is "a movement without a cause":

> Despite rapid growth, there are still not enough machines in one classroom to trigger reform in large-group instructional patterns — to which the microcomputer, with its almost intimate relationship to the individual user, is not well suited.

The assumption of inevitable one-on-oneness is hardware-driven, as are most of our great expectations. In this case our imagination is confounded by a view of hardware at once obsolete and implausibly futuristic. We have dragged into a present full of cheap, portable microcomputers a notion of how to relate to the computers of twenty years ago, the huge and fantastically expensive machines whose use (efficiency was the watchword) had to be tightly restricted. While this notion is no longer up-to-date, we have clung to an instructional style geared to such restricted use, assuming, unimaginitively, that the problems we're experiencing with CAI are merely transitional and will dissolve when we have enough of those plentiful micros for everyone. It is as if we had to compensate for the discomfort of scarcity — just as parents having lived through the Depression are fiercely determined that their children have tangible savings — by attempting to provide each child with the advantage we didn't have as children, of sitting in front of his very own computer, studying with his very own CAI program.

This is neither pedagogically sound nor a realistic use of resources. Failing to provide all but the most simplistic dialogue, and that with an anonymous screen, CAI enforces the habits of isolation that are counterproductive to most forms of learning. It does nothing to facilitate communication with other human beings, with teachers and fellow learners. Quite the contrary, it poses as an ideal the doing away with such communication. The single greatest hope people have for CAI is that in due time it will provide truly individualized instruction tailored automatically to the student as though it had sensors tracking eye twitching and skin temperature. This is an illusion. CAI may have complex branching programs and increasingly sophisticated prescriptive instruction (although very few current programs even promise that much) but the one thing it will not be is individualized in any useful, intimate sense. It also cannot and will not be able to stimulate experimentation — action, transformation, accumulation of experience of one's self as both a learner and a contributor to the world. These failings are probably in our best interest, for as soon as we start making software that runs itself, educators and students alike lose all control.

That use of the one-on-one format is problematic is acknowledged far and wide. What is not appreciated is the foolhardiness of a remedy involving more machines and more CAI software. The problem is more profound than insufficient resources, although that matter must force us to question whether it makes sense to spend $20,000 on a handful of micros over a flesh-and-blood teacher, or to allow history to be elbowed out of the way by subjects more susceptible to quantification. If, in an ideal world, we could provide enough computer-aided instruction to go around, we would still have a problem. For CAI cannot teach. It can only dispense facts which alone have very little to do with learning. And it can dispense those facts only in series, like a string of beads, without the critical contextual patterns, without genuine dialogue. The result is ungrounded, unmemorable learning as likely to fly out of the student's mind as those beads are to snap under tension and go spilling across the floor.

One-on-one instruction also puts undue stress on the already frayed social fabric of the class. Resembling the isolated environment of the home, the model is fundamentally inconsistent with schooling which is, by design, the instruction of groups of children gathered together to learn. School is school, after all, not home writ large. Its classrooms, its 25:1 student-to-teacher ratio, its most basic systems militate against the CAI approach — against any approach for that matter, including programming, which presupposes an intimate relationship between the computer and the individual user.

It is of course true that each child has different interests and abilities, and that each one needs individual attention. It is also true that a school activity — a session with the speech therapist or an advanced math tutorial — that singles out one child or a few is disruptive and potentially discriminatory. Imagine what it would be like if the child actually had a private tutor who sat with him at a special desk, doing specially individualized lessons. That child certainly might learn some extra things (though probably due more to the human contact than the tutorial format itself), but he would be deprived of contact with his peers, who would in their turn be justifiably resentful of his special treatment. Special treatment is what the computer offers with current CAI. Unintentionally though inevitably, CAI also tends to reinforce the pattern in which children identified as bright and dull are thrust out of the amorphous middle and into their respective limelights. Which children do CAI? The younger kids, the ones considered dull, and the urban minorities.

If we choose to employ this style of software throughout the entire curriculum, we may create a situation where student isolation is increasingly intense, the social fabric (what there is of it) further damaged, and the already strained relationship between teacher and student further disrupted by the intervening technology.

The Good News

There is some good news, though all of it equivocal. The mode for the masses, CAI turns out to be appropriate for only a few, and not necessarily the ones who are getting it. Students highly motivated to learn a narrowly defined, partitionable, fact- or procedure-based subject may find CAI useful, at least for short bursts. They will want to be able to control the time they spend learning by this method, and to alternate with other, more socially interactive styles. They may find it a convenience, like a washing machine, in that it relieves some of the tedium of rote learning; this depends on the quality of the software. The novelty of it wears off too quickly to be educationally significant. Whether CAI is valuable in freeing students to pursue more challenging studies depends on what they do with the extra time.

Students doing remedial work may appreciate the patience of the drillmaster and the clarity, if it is so designed, with which the material is presented. This again is a function of software quality. The material may not be clear (it is bound to be limited), the rewards and punishments may be inappropriate, even rude, and the learning experience every bit as flat as paper-and-pencil drill.

Kids doing specialized study at a rate either faster or slower than their classmates may also find CAI advantageous. Location of the computer, scheduling of time on-line, support from teachers, and the opportunity to learn by other methods all influence the extent to which self-paced instruction is a help or a hindrance.

CAI can be attractive, though it rarely is. Fancy graphics and catchy tunes can be used constructively, for conveying information supportive of the text or enhancing the quality of interaction, but all too often they are poorly utilized. Too often are merely decorated CAI programs billed as games, thereby prompting kids to expect that they be fun, that they have a game's sense-making rules and that playing be a satisfying challenge. Children are not fooled by the graphics and the tunes, but bored — perhaps even more than they would have been by frankly boring studies — and rightfully annoyed at being manipulated.

CAI may also have marginal utility in building confidence with computers among the timid, for it is, on the surface, the easiest software to use and certainly the most familiar, its content drawn straight from the pages of basic textbooks. Attacks on CAI have prompted many educators to rise to its defense, saying, "Hey! Be realistic. There's a world out here and a lot of us who like CAI." Their anxiety is talking, not their pedagogical vision, for it turns out that they're not really using CAI on a significant scale. Since CAI is the only software they understand, they're willing to say the stuff is OK.

But even its ease of use is deceptive. CAI places terrible demands on the teacher, who must now fill in the information gaps, provide reinforcement, clarification and context bridges, and satisfy student needs for simple human interaction. All this for the one or two or five kids in the CAI contingent having their turn at the computer. The rest must be taught and attended to in the low-tech fashion. Would it be better if there were machines for all? Not likely, just fantastically more expensive.

A school is an interlocking set of 25-to-30-kid classrooms, and it may not make sense for every one of those classrooms to be converted to a 30-ring computer circus. We must continually ask whether the price is worth it in the context of overall educational priorities, if it makes sense to attempt to provide for all a style of instruction appropriate only for a few, and whether — if we do choose to employ this method to help us teach the subjects it can handle — we want our children to learn what CAI teaches about learning.

6.

Mind Tools and Other Fine Things

TO PETAL
QCIRCLE 50
RIGHT 90
QCIRCLE 50
RIGHT 90
END

TO NEWFLOWER
REPEAT 10)
    PETAL
    RIGHT 360/10
END

TO PLANT
NEWFLOWER
BACK 50
PETAL
BACK 50
END

MORSE CODE
100 CALL CLEAR
110 PRINT TAB(7);"*********
    ****"
120 PRINT TAB(7);"* MORSE
    CODE *"
130 PRINT TAB(7);"*********
    *****":: ::
140 CALL CHAR(37,:3C7EFFF
    FFFFF7E3C")
150 CALL CHAR(38,"00FFFF
    FFFFFFFF")
160 DIM M$(35),N(35)
170 FOR A=0 TO 35
180 READ M$(A)
190 NEXT A
200 DATA &&&&&,%&&&&,
    %%&&&,%%%&&,%%%&
210 DATA %%%%,&%%%%,
    &&%%%,&&&%%,&&&&%

```
220 DATA %&,&%%%,&%&%,
    &%%,%,%%&%,&&%
230 DATA %%%%,%%,%&&&,
    &%&,%&%%,&&,&%
```

The computer-as-tool approach to educational computing represents a more interesting application than CAI, though one that is no less problematic. The category includes programming languages such as LOGO and BASIC, illustrated above, as well as word processing and numerical analysis. Its unifying element is a relationship quite different from that found in computer-aided instruction. If the purpose of CAI is to teach (or "program") the child, here the computer is the learner. The computer is programmed (or "taught") by the child to do something useful or delightful or otherwise desirable.

How refreshing are the messages one gets *about learning* when using the computer as a tool! Here is a puzzle to be studied from different angles, like a wonderfully complex sculpture. Solving the puzzle involves choosing not the correct among the incorrect but the best of several plausible alternatives. What's more, those alternative solutions — sometimes the puzzle itself — are creatures of one's own invention. The learner poses the question (the computer is the respondent) and shapes the twisty path to the answer.

Thinking It Over on the Razor's Edge

Advocates argue that in learning to program, children learn to understand their own ways of thinking and learning. We all know how easy it is to be smug about one's facility with a procedure, particularly something used so often it has become second nature. Think of balancing a checkbook or tying a shoe. Think of walking! It's easy right? (A tap on the forehead with the middle two fingers: "It's all in here, in the old noggin.") But try to explain how it's done to another person — explain it verbally or in writing, not by demonstration — and one may discover with dismay that all was not so crystal clear in the old noggin. Trying to explain it to a computer is worse, for to program one must communicate in excruciatingly literal programming languages.

In having to articulate those habits and understandings, one is forced to know them more thoroughly — at least, more procedurally — than one did before. The computer has no room for ambiguity, no artful or instinctive skill in filling in lapses in the specification. Writes Frederick Brooks in *The Mythical Man-Month*, "If one character, one pause, of the incantation is not strictly in proper form, the magic doesn't work."

The programmer is thus in ardent pursuit of perfection — a particular kind, whose parameters define the program. But he can, paradoxically, seek his goal within a highly flexible, resilient, even forgiving environment. Unlike CAI, with its black-and-white right or wrongness, programming offers the uninhibiting opportunity to see "bugs" — the little critters that stand in the way of the magic and that in another pedagogical system would be classified as "wrong" — as intriguing puzzles in and of themselves, peepholes into the nature of the larger puzzle one is working on. To the programmer, this puzzle can be infinitely fascinating, in part due to its complexity but more importantly because it is his creation. It is earth, air, fire, and water.

Those who practice the craft enjoy its paradoxical nature in many different ways. There are those whose deepest thrill is the walk on the razor's edge (one slip and the magic crashes the program) and those who are freed to do their work on the computer — writing, graphics, math, design, whatever — by its grant of enormous latitude in fixing bugs, typos, miscalculations. There are those whose programming style is a total immersion in mathematical waters, like a Berlitz language course, and those who do it for the beauty of the patterns, the pictures, and the dancing color. All must ultimately be precise, but the risk of being wrong is no obstacle to learning. "The question to ask about the program," writes Papert,

> is not whether it is right or wrong, but if it is fixable. If this way of looking at intellectual products were generalized to

how the larger culture thinks about knowledge and its acquisition, we might be less intimidated by our fears of "being
wrong."

Barrier-free Learning

Papert makes the case that teaching methods which require the
rote learning of rules and procedures associated with subjects
themselves tightly defined not only inhibit curiosity and experimentation, and thereby the free flow of learning, but act to
divide children prematurely into specialties. Intellectual
strength breeds intellectual weakness, just as one might favor a
"good" eye and let the weaker one slide. The computer is potentially so multipurposeful a tool as to offer children coming
from all directions a chance to learn in new barrier-free ways,
and to learn subjects freed from the bonds of rigid definition.

A child working with LOGO is drawing complex geometrical
shapes on the screen. Asked what she is doing, she replies "I'm
drawing," and so she is, taking in at the same time the no longer
bitter pill of mathematics. A child who in the past may have
hated math and science (or spelling or writing or reading) is
now able to approach these subjects gladly. The computer, that
most responsive machine, lets him make of math or grammar
something that makes sense and that is more in line with his
natural forms of expression.

Educators greet these developments with enthusiasm, happy
to endorse whatever can open children's minds so naturally to
powerful ideas. Many schools have tried LOGO, and most have
found that kids love it and seem to learn all kinds of exciting
things from fooling around with it. It seems to be wonderful
stuff, and perhaps only the first chink in a breakthrough made
possible by the presence of computers in the classroom.

But let's not forget that despite its delightful aspects, LOGO,
like other types of programming, is fundamentally an analytical
activity in which the challenge is to divide such things as images
or processes into their component parts and put them back
together in functioning order. It may be inappropriate to em-
phasize this mode at such an early age. Let's also not forget that

LOGO is a tool, and therefore has no built-in rules or pointers to intellectual domains. It is a kind of electronic skateboard which kids can use to get someplace, but they need an impetus to start them on the way and contact with a teacher to keep them going forward. LOGO may enliven the creative process. It may integrate traditionally segregated subjects. But it does not convey information or inspire cognitive development. What it does is enhance the way children use the cognitive abilities they possess.

The little formal research that has been done in comparing the efficacy of LOGO to CAI offers mild support to this conclusion. One test, conducted by Douglas H. Clements at Kent State University and reported in *Electronic Learning*, split a group of first graders into a LOGO programming group and a CAI control group, keeping the same teachers for each. The results of the Torrance Test, which measures a child's ability to think creatively when drawing, showed significant differences in the areas of fluency, originality, and overall creativity. The LOGO group dramatically increased its scores while the group doing CAI, which emphasizes not creativity but getting the right answer, showed no significant increase. Results were comparable in the Matching Familiar Figures Test of reflectivity, indicating that LOGO may encourage children to think problems through while CAI may prompt them to leap to answers without much thought. No differences were found between the two groups in the areas of cognitive development and logical thinking.

Project Zero's Perkins compares LOGO unfavorably with practice-intensive direct strategies (learn, practice, apply, repeat) at least in the "sandbox style" of learning which leaves kids to their own devices in the absence of active instructional intervention. Kids "in the sandbox" will play with LOGO up to a point, just as with Lego blocks or Tinker Toys — to a ceiling, apparently, on their cognitive development beyond which they do not move, week after week, without either outside guidance or the fluky impetus of extreme enthusiasm.

Intervention works with anything. If a teacher or parent is active in helping the child make connections, in clarifying ideas, encouraging practice of the skill or knowledge, LOGO, Lego, direct instruction — anything — is effective. So is extraordinary enthusiasm such as might be felt for the violin by a musical prodigy. Such enthusiasm is a powerful learning aid insofar as it may lead the student to spend an extraordinary length of time learning. Almost all sophisticated performances spring not from the gifted brow of one of the gods but from terrific effort and much, much more "time-on-task" than that devoted to other subjects. A LOGO-saturated, high intervention environment is thus likely to get results. Likewise, a school that can afford to offer its students unfettered reign in other programming activities, and to support those activities with some lively teaching, may find those students becoming increasingly skillful in that particular mode. Is this so valuable as to be worth the expense and the forfeiting of other studies?

Beyond the Sandbox

The focus of programming activity in schools shifts to other languages and other goals when the kids get past age ten or so. It is the second most popular application of computers in education. Trained to program, children are supposed to think more clearly and logically, and be more adept at problem solving. This may be true within a limited set of definitions of "think" and "problem" and "solve," and it may be true for some children. But computer-oriented problem solving and logical thinking are not universally applicable skills. Neither does programming necessarily teach precise thinking, for it is every bit as possible to write a sloppy program as it is to write a sloppy essay.

Programming is also supposed to prepare our children for the job market and for post-secondary education. Does this make sense? Is it even feasible? The needs of business and industry are changing at a rate much faster than schools can adapt to, so fast that what is most up-to-the-minute when Johnny is shuffling his way through high school may be passé by the time he is looking for work. Anyway, most schools do not teach programming in C or assembly language or something else that might be useful, but in BASIC, which thrives nowhere but the schools and the livingrooms of those rugged souls willing, either through stubbornness or naïveté, to put up with its limitations.

It might be more efficient for the kid to take a quickie course at a local college when and if he's ready to learn a computer language, when he has a clue what to learn and why he should learn it, and when he has a prayer of being able to put it to use. Even this moderate approach may backfire, however. In the wake of devastating layoffs and forced "vacations" at many Boston-area high-tech firms, the *Boston Globe* reported in June 1985,

> Specialists in the field of vocational education are warning that new crash programs being mounted by state and local governments across the country to train a bumper crop of "high technicians" risk creating a glut on the labor market, with such predictable long-term impacts as depressing the wages of the most recently educated and contributing to the promotion of frustrated expectations.

Since developments in the technological realm have been notoriously unpredictable over the years, it cannot be said that children need to become computer programmers — or computer literates, or even to have their lessons computer-aided — with any more confidence than that they do not. For the run-of-the-mill user, programming is no more critical to running a computer than tuning engines is to running a car. One does not have to write a computer program in order to use a computer any more than one needs to write a TV program to use a television, or write a novel to read a book. We have learned to use cars and televisions incidently, as we needed or wanted to make use of those devices. The pervasiveness of a technology is thus not in itself a sufficient argument for knowing about it, certainly not for turning the school pocketbook inside out to teach it.

How much more sensible is the following approach, offered by Beverly Hunter, president of Targeted Learning, a Virginia-based company developing educational materials for schools. Phrased as a definition of computer literacy, it is equally applicable to the issue of programming.

> Computer literacy is whatever a person needs to be able to know about and do with computers in order to function ef-

fectively in our information-based society. This definition points out that what skills and knowledges and attitudes are needed will vary from person to person and from time to time, depending on what it is they are doing. This definition also points out that computers are tools in the service of other work — not an end in themselves.

For some children programming may have vocational merit, and it should be offered to these kids — if trained instructors can be induced to stay in teaching — as an optional vocational subject. Students should be cautioned, however, against assuming that the training has ready value in the marketplace. For some it may serve the general purpose of helping to increase prolem-solving and logic skills, though this too should be understood as having less than universal application. Programming should be one small, optional element in the panoply of skills and knowledge our children need to go out into the world as full human beings; as walking, talking, thinking, working, responsive, and responsible adults.

Hand Tools

In programming, the computer is used as a tool-making tool — at its best a "mind-tool" with which children can invent their own intellectual structures and aids to thinking. The computer-as-tool has other, more humble applications of some utility in education and beyond, particularly as a word processor and a tool for numerical analysis. Most of these general purpose tools were not created as instructional devices, but have been appropriated to help school children write and "crunch numbers" more efficiently and more effectively than they could without them.

Some general purpose tools are used straight, some piggybacked with other instructional modes — a CAI rider on VisiCalc, for example, to provide start-up instruction in how to use that spreadsheet program. Or word processing programs augmented with spelling aids or other special features, such as note card mini-programs or sentence structure reviews, designed to help improve writing style and organization. Advanced word processors of this sort have been hailed as "idea processors," blessing the harried writer with the equivalent of divine guidance by fostering the good thinking that precedes good writing and easing the pain of composition.

Whether or not these miracles come to pass, it is true that word processing (and to a lesser extent, numerical analysis) can be used to advantage across the board — in the study of virtually every subject or vocational area. There are drawbacks, however, and factors that should give pause. A word processor may make typing as easy as falling off a log, but it has no inherent ability to transform an ill-conceived, badly written essay into something fine. Fans claim that with word processors it is so much easier to make major revisions to a document that, for the first time, kids are willing to do more than tack on a sentence or two to their first draft. But most of the editing people do on word processors is within the local realm of sentences modified and paragraphs cut and pasted. When all but 25 eighty-character lines are concealed behind the impassive screen, one may have less of a global sense of the content, structure, and overall quality of a piece several pages in length than if those several pages were spread across a desk and allowed to mingle with real cardboard note cards, ashtrays, sticky cups, and eraser fuzz. At least one can see it there, out in the open. Without the screen-priest to mediate, there is a physical immediacy to one's relationship with the writing that may — for some writers, at some stages of the writing process — be preferable to the sanitary, high-technological method.

As with all educational applications of computers, we must ask of word processing and the other tools: is it worth it? It would require enormous amounts of time and space — both human and computer — to make general purpose tools available to every student. Still more to integrate such tool use into the normal workings of the school, so that word processing, for example, was an integral part of an English composition class. Since wide access is unlikely, we're left with the usual widening gaps between schools that have and those that have not, between students who get it in school or do not, and between students who have the advantage of a word processor at home and those who do not.

Made in Vermont

The computer-as-tool may be more intriguing than it is educationally useful, at least insofar as it is currently applied. Its popularity, usually justified in terms of the job market and cognition, reflects a deeper, age-old fascination with tools, including the process by which they are made and by which people use them to make other things.

When in the early seventies Saab introduced the team approach to car making, people who had previously limited their car talk to miles per gallon found it fascinating that the engine in their gleaming new 99 had been assembled, not on a line but by a tight-knit squad of Swedish artisans. It was partly the sense that the car was handmade that was so engaging. One could imagine tracing the car's origins, starting with the serial number and plowing through Saab records to find the date and time it emerged from the line and the names of the team members. Get autographs, maybe. Do the car's astrological chart. It was also exciting, in focusing so intimately on the car-making process, to realize that this process directly influenced the quality of the end product.

Computers have brought with them a revival of the same interest in craft. We are discovering that the computer tools we work with are essentially handmade, by people we can read about in popular magazines. We have also discovered that we can do it ourselves. They awaken that part of us that wants to give up fast food and grid-locked commuting for a blacksmith shop in Vermont, where we could wear leather smocks and say, with dignity, "I'm a toolmaker."

When a handmade tool is good, it's very good. It is integrated into human life, and has the technological equivalent of smooth, solid handles that fit well into human hands. Like the hand itself, it is perfectly balanced between maximum flexibility and appropriateness for its intended application. Such tools are hard to find, harder still to make for oneself, for development is a painstakingly long process, more an art than a science. The successful development of fundamental tools — think of the wheel, or television — is often the work of several generations.

We have a lot to learn about the computer-as-tool. It may be that, as with CAI, its utility is not quite where we expect it to be. Some of the benefits may simply be in the pleasure we find in making things and in joining the new crowd of technological craftspeople. It may also be that the appropriate audience for computers may be other than we had thought.

A Good Tool Is Hard to Find

Chalk is a metaphor currently in wide use among designers and other advocates of educational computer-tools. It is a strong image, evoking an instinctive and instantaneous favorable response. "Yes!" chimes the populace, "we'd love it if computers could be as accessible and easy to use as a piece of chalk." It is an image that extends beyond mere word processing to encompass virtually all of what we hope will be technology's educational roles and all the ways we expect it to make learning more effective, more interesting, and better suited to the needs of individual learners. The idea of software chalk is also appealing because it sounds like a tool for teachers who are, after all, the chief users of real dust-on-the-fingers chalk.

Collectively, the nation bends over backwards to make sure our children have hands-on exposure to computers, whether through CAI or the tool approaches such as LOGO, BASIC programming, word processing. Our hearts are in the right place — we want to help children learn — but our narrow focus on the kids may be getting in the way of our helping them. It is the very exclusivity of CAI and tools that makes these approaches ineffective in the classroom. Both are too demanding of the teacher to allow him to take care of an entire class, and neither can function as intended due to problems of access to too-few machines.

It was hard to admit these failures just a short while ago, when zealots pressed for "power to the kids" with late-sixties single-mindedness. We were convinced that software, like Trix, was for kids. Teachers may have experimented with a grading program or other such administrative aid, but when the experts said, "Turn the computer around," it seemed selfish not to do so. It seemed that those administrative uses were somehow less legitimate than the expressly educational applications. And who were teachers to object, anyway? What did they know about handling computers? Teachers are often plagued by insecurity about their teaching abilities. As Holt says, every teacher's fear is that administrators will find out what really goes on in his classroom. This insecurity left them ripe for gurus and gimmicks, and vulnerable to the directives about computers, which contain elements of both.

Perhaps now that we've acknowledged some of the disappointment, we can consider the possibility that we're not ready to grab hold of the "intimate machine" so intimately. Perhaps we should acknowledge that design and implementation of workable software for single child/machine units is too difficult at this stage in the revolution. Consider instead that this may be the time to focus on software chalk *for the teacher* as a more appropriate application in the second half of the 1980s. Something they can use in all the ways they use chalk — for everything from lesson plans to diagramming sentences, and from making lists of kids who still owe homework to illustrating Neptune's orbital path around the sun.

The school-age population rises and falls and the numbers of teachers are adjusted accordingly — this notwithstanding the onslaught of technology, for however available school computers may become, they cannot and will not replace teachers. We can therefore expect to continue to have solitary teachers confronted by groups of twenty to thirty students in each classroom, and that teacher thus in charge of the learning environment and how the technology is used. Despite the popularity of the chalk metaphor, there is almost no real software chalk on the market aside from a handful of programs to help teachers write reports, grade papers, compose worksheets. For kids, there are technological "pencils" as big as a horse's leg and word processors that, delightful as they may be in integrating words with sound and graphics, are unavoidably limited by the usual difficulties associated with use in a classroom with twenty-five kids, one teacher, and scant funds. What is designed directly to support the teacher's classroom activities? Virtually nothing. There may be — there must be! — ways to use the computer as a dedicated tool for teachers.

What could it be? Imagine. A monitor would sit on the teacher's desk, facing her, belonging, as do the files and report books, to her, not the children. Imagine that the images on this screen would be for Teachers Eyes Only, though they needn't be; they could be amplified via one large screen (there are such devices) or several smaller screens positioned such that everyone could see. Delivery would suddenly be one small fraction of the problem it was with child-centered hardware and software.

The teacher would have access to software chalk as diverse as the uses of the real thing. She could use it administratively, and without apology, for this application would no longer be antithetical to the broad purposes of educational software. Grading programs, report writers, database managers, classroom filers — all would be as easy to use as the sophisticated multi-purpose business programs are today. The teacher, of course, could also use it as a teaching tool, drawing on simulations, games, direct instruction, and programs to support class discussion. Different teachers would use the different types of software according to their needs and teaching styles, some with zesty imagination, others, step-by-step. Still others might not use the computer at all, software chalk or no software chalk, either out of reluctance, possibly fear, or because they did not need to.

When genuine software chalk is invented, it should come, like any good tool, in response to organic needs. It should have the equivalent of smooth wooden handles, and be comfortably integrated in the life of the classroom without demanding drastic change. Since the key elements are still the teacher, the kids, and the environment they create together, use of software chalk should follow that lead, follow the distinct styles of individual teachers and each, unique class.

7.

It's How You Play the Game

The left side of the room, by the bookshelves and the pin-wheels, was a flat plain of the Peloponnesus. A series of runners brought shocking rumors of the Athenian confrontation with Corinth. Near the blackboard, the Spartan council worriedly debated its alternatives. Over by the windows, the Athenians gathered to calculate the Spartan response. Supplies and resources had to be allocated; decisions that could alter the course of history had to be made and made quickly. The runners left again, carrying urgent messages to allies....

Classroom simulations like this are not new. Model United Nations's have been around for years, conducted in high school gymnasiums throughout the country with only hand-lettered cardboard signs for props saying "Chad" and "Korea" and "U.S.S.R." Forever, it would seem, have kids learned "economics" by running lemonade stands and car washes, and in science class they've observed patterns of plant growth by simulating night and day with a closet and a sun lamp. What is new is the participation of computers in classroom simulations and games, where the computer is used to model a "microworld" — a dynamic metaphor of some slice of reality, complete with data about events within the microworld and preprogrammed rules

governing the interaction of those events. Computer-based simulations are typically used to emulate natural systems, axiomatic
mathematical systems, socio-polical systems, and business systems. The goals are the promotion of skill mastery, concept
development, and student inquiry in an environment which, it
is hoped, will be so engaging as to provide its own motivations
to learn.

A simulation is not a jumble of facts and variables but a model,
limited by definition and technology, and designed by virtue of
those limitations to focus student attention on certain aspects of
the thing under study. Suspending disbelief as they would at
the theater, students enter the world of the simulation to explore
its nooks and crannies and chasms and to test hypotheses about
problems they encounter by manipulating environmental variables. It is a guided form of trial and error intensified by the
powerful presence of the computer, yet at the same time made
safer by that very technology, which allows one to try and to err
without risk of losing more than a turn.

Simulations can also be games, for the game world is a simulated environment. It is often less literal than that of a classroom simulation but it has, like a simulation, its own internal
consistency, and offers similar opportunities to learn. Fun is the
chief motivator in learning games. It is intended to set off a
chain reaction — from fun to motivating to a greater likelihood
that children will learn the concepts and skills interwoven within
the play fabric of the game. Computer-based learning games
range from those which might more accurately be called drills,
where the superficial features of gaming are added purely as
motivational devices, to games representing wonderfully complex and content-rich environments. The format holds tremendous potential — perhaps the most of any educational use of
computers — including the possibility that we can convert the
quintessentially non-human computer into something quite
human.

Serious Business

Learning games and simulations are the least well utilized form
of computer-supported or computer-oriented learning in the

schools. One of the major obstacles to their use is the very fact of their being fun to play, which by a straight-laced line of reasoning is suspected as incompatible with learning, or at least to crowd the sort of learning that should take precedence. "You don't get through high school by being a good games player," asserts one educational software publisher who favors CAI. "You get through high school by having good grades."

Unarticulated goals represent another shortcoming. As Sherwin Steffin, now president of Brainworks, an educational software company, said in a July 1984 interview:

> The chief problem with [some] educational games is that the instructional goals are unclear. Because of that, they cannot be evaluated and it's uncertain whether the goals have ever been achieved.

The game component is seen as competitive with the educational content and, to the extent that it takes up valuable program space and learning time, actually detrimental. Besides, school children are a captive audience and therefore do not *have* to be enticed with fun-coated learning. Unlike their brothers and sisters at home, who simply will not bother with unappealing software, kids in school have little choice in what they're taught, or how.

There is little room for learning games and simulations in an educational system dedicated exclusively to transmission of the explicit skills and content that comprise the formal curriculum. But by insisting on such explicit goals as the passport to school software legitimacy, we neglect the unarticulated informal curriculum, especially learning to be gained from interpersonal relations. Confounded by the slippery immeasurability of games, we also fail to appreciate their strength in conveying the content and skills we so highly regard. The school system pressed to get results may think that games are very well and good in their place, but it cannot afford to use unverifiable methods. We cannot risk not knowing exactly what our instructional efforts produce." These days, education has neither the resources nor the inclination to acknowledge the value of social skills or the power of social interaction in fostering other kinds of learning.

The Mythical Measurable Medium

Our efforts to use computers to get back to basics are founded on the insubstantial promise of measurability, a promise held out by the technology itself like the air-drawn dagger in front of Macbeth. "Captivated by our psedo-scientific capacity to measure things," writes Olds in "The Microcomputer and the Hidden Curriculum," "we have assumed that what is important in education is what is obvious and easily measurable." We're chasing our own tail here, reasoning further that what is measurable is important and that, since (we think) computers offer measurable instruction, they're just the thing to help us get where we're going.

A digital medium (one/zero; on/off), software seems to lend itself to quantitative applications — in education, to no-nonsense drill-and-practice (yes/no; true/false) — and for that reason among others, has been adopted by the movement to convert education into likewise measurable units. Ask someone with a digital watch, "Hey, you know what time it is?" and you won't get a nicely rounded "quarter-to-four" but rather, in clipped tones, "It is three forty-seven." Ask a computer to be a tireless drone, to dispense, monitor, and evaluate CAI, and it will do just that without complaint and without leaving a shred of ambiguity about whether Sammy has conquered his seven-times-sevens. This dogged drill-and-practice capability is used because it's there and because it satisfies current requirements. It satisfies at least the superficial needs of schools under pressure to raise SAT scores, to *do something* in response to the revelation that one out of every five Americans is a functional illiterate.

> A man walking down a city street at night comes upon a fellow crouched under a street lamp.
>
> "I've lost my keys," says the crouching man.
>
> "Where did you lose them?" asks the other.
>
> "Over there, in that dark driveway."
>
> "Then why are you looking for them here?"
>
> "Because it's light here."

This is what we have done with software. We have looked in the easiest, most readily measurable places for the solution to our educational needs. Have we found it with CAI? No. With LOGO? Sort of.

Although the CAI approach has yet to be proven effective (all we know is that it's wildly expensive and unpardonably difficult to use), it has become the standard against which other software is compared. Learning games must now be defended, preposterously, in terms of results achieved. Educators are straining to set quantitative standards for a form that defies quantification, and educational game developers are scrambling to make their products fit within those awkward criteria. This is a waste and an unfruitful accomodation to a collective imagination that has not kept pace with the new medium, but sees it only in terms of automating current teaching practices in the service of the formal curriculum. The decontextualization of games by this too-close scrutiny of their educational product overlooks, like the forest for the trees, their tremendous educational potency. We must be willing to grope in the dark, to admit that not everything worthwhile is measurable and not everything measurable is worthwhile.

What's in a Game?

A game is an *interactional activity* played by one or more players, either competitively or collaboratively, according to a set of agreed-upon rules which define the content of the game and which include criteria for determining the winner. It is above all supposed to be fun to play. Games have been an important medium for informal learning for as long as there have been people to play them. It is on the basis of their traditional strength and delightfulness that educational computer games have been created. Let us take a look at games in general — not high-tech, particularly, or intentionally educational — to understand their function and their power.

Most games serve three general educational purposes: to incorporate and disseminate cultural values, attitudes, and beliefs; to provide a free atmosphere for participants to experience, initiate, discuss, devise, and change the rules for social interaction; and to promote the development of contextually-based skills, both physical and conceptual.

Games are not biological or ecological universals. They are cultural inventions, rather, their contours reflecting the interactive styles and mores of the particular cultures in which they are played. In their seminal 1959 article, "Games in Culture," social anthropologists John Roberts, Malcolm Arth, and Robert Bush classified games according to patterns of play, differentiating between games of physical skill, strategy, and chance. Games of physical skill, whose outcomes are determined by players' physical abilities, are typically models of combat (e.g., boxing) or hunting (trap shooting) activities. Games of strategy such as chess or backgammon are often models of war. Their outcomes are a function of the players' choices in a series of considered moves. Games of chance (gambling, the lottery) are models of divining reflective of a culture's views of the supernatural. Outcomes here, undirected by human volition, are the result of non-rational guessing or the operation of a mechanical chance device such as a die or roulette wheel.

Games are thus miniature control systems embedded in the macroscopic systems of the culture. They also have a part in shaping the culture, for each wave of players makes little changes here and there, adapting the games to suit its perceptions of a changing world, and thereby alters the very patterns along which that world develops.

Joining in the Fun

Whatever the format, games give children the interactional experiences upon which socialization turns. The centuries-old pattern begins with children sitting on their parents' laps; listening and learning as the parent reads stories, plays patty cake-patty cake-baker's man, and puts together marvelous (non-computer) simulations with colored paper, crayon, and sticky tape. This is the original meaning of "interaction" — inter-*human*-action.

At first, the parent plays to, or at, the child. The child responds, mimics, and eventually joins in the play. The quality of interaction with parents, at this first stage and throughout childhood, is determined in large part by the parents' capacity to consider the child a person with valid needs and worthy contributions to make. It is also a matter of gearing that interaction to a level appropriate to each child. When Dad takes his favorite toddler outdoors to introduce him to baseball, he should start by rolling the ball on the ground, not by playing nine innings. The main thing is the lap learning. Everything else is gravy.

As a child gets a little older she turns inward toward solitary, imaginitive play. She can be found on the floor of her room or sprawled on a grassy incline, talking in a swarm of voices, not to herself, but, to a cast of characters invisible to the casual observer but indisputibly vivid, even palpable, to the child. She is beginning to learn to play at different roles. Although she is alone, her play-world is crowded with characters interacting with one another, being pals, punitive, sweet, mean, cajoling, solicitous, sad, glad.

The child returns in time to play with others, now more with playmates — siblings and other friends — than with parents. This peer interaction is another requirement for the adequate development of social sensitivity. The limited research that has been done on the subject indicates that children without such contact fall behind in their ability to put themselves in someone else's shoes. Child development researchers M. Hollos and P. A. Cowan studied seven- to nine-year-olds from three Norwegian settings — a town, a village, and a dispersed farming community in the Arctic tundra. Children from this third group rarely left home before school age (eight years) except for major holidays and family occasions. Their interactions were confined to within the family, mainly to one or two siblings. These children scored the lowest of the three groups in measures of their ability to report what another person would see, to repeat a story to someone who had never heard it before, and to take the role of storyteller in a cartoon-picture sequence.

Although it may be that such role-taking skills were less than essential to adult life in the tundra, and that play experiences for these children were as reflective of their culture as what goes on on the playing fields of Eton is for the winner at Waterloo, in most parts of the modern world the ability to put oneself in another's shoes is undeniably a critical skill. The exercise is something most children take to naturally. They crave social interaction, and unless something or someone interferes, they find ways to be with people, either directly or in parallel play.

The Joy of Foosball

Television (alias the electronic babysitter) interrupted the ancient interaction patterns. Now the kids spend eight hours a day in front of the tube, plugged into what is a fundamentally passive activity. "Sesame Street," one of the few exceptions, is about as interactive as TV can be — children sing with it, dance with it, fetch their own truck when one appears on the screen. In that sense, "Sesame Street" transcends TV. It is also exceptionally non-linear. The audience need not stay glued to the set to follow a story line, but can wander in and out of other parallel activities. But television typically demands a fixated passivity from its viewers, compensating for the lack of interactive engagement with tremendously rich program content. Contrast this with the much thinner content of video games. It would be tedious to watch a game of PacMan or Zaaxon without being able to participate in some fashion, if only as a fan.

"Television is something you watch," writes Turkle. "Games are something you do." Video games thus bring us and our children a few steps closer to the original pattern. We call them interactive in generous acknowledgment of the involvement between player and machine, and the greater this involvement the more entertaining we regard the program.

Interactivity of this type is possibly the most inflated concept of the 1980s. The current level of interaction between humans and machines doesn't come close to a ten-minute conversation with a perfect stranger. It's pathetic, relatively. It's prehistoric. And it does nothing to satisfy the deep human need to be with other people, to respond to them and work with them toward a common goal.

Parents often notice to their dismay that a video game purchased for the home has nothing like the same appeal as the identical game at the arcade parlor. The stakes are lower at home, for one thing. There's a quarter (or several) at stake at the arcade, and that makes the game much more exciting. There is also a certain magnetism about a place where other kids are playing, an attraction more compelling than the marginal draw of even "interactive" software played at home, in solitude and against a backdrop of domestic noise.

Arcade parlors are thus the site of a curiously hybrid form of social/non-social interaction, for while the kids are playing one-on-one with the games, their buddies are hanging over their shoulder, shouting and groaning along with the game's ups and downs. It's like dancing in the second half of the twentieth century, with dancers wanting other dancers nearby, but not to touch.

The following scene was observed one night at a video arcade in a mid-sized coastal town. The walls were black, as one would expect, the lighting electric blue and fuchsia, and the sounds that wierd, synthesized mix of crashing and beeping. Two dozen video games were lined up along the wall, *but no one was playing them*. Instead, perhaps fifteen kids were engaged in a passionate game of "foosball" — a game dating back to their grandfathers' time and involving no microchips or LEDs whatsoever, nor, for that matter, any quarters. Four kids were energetically twisting the sticks, slamming a hard little ball back and forth and occasionally through the goal posts. The rest were playing the old spectator game of cheering on the players.

It is almost as if, side by side with the desire for increasingly high-tech games, people have a contrary desire to lower the technology in order to make the game-playing more social. Low-tech games, almost by definition, include at least two players, and the more, in many cases, the merrier. Even a dopey game like Chutes & Ladders can be fun with a group, although adults may want to bring along a couple of beers. It matters far more that there be people nearby — to play with, to watch and be watched by — than that the game be technologically sophisticated.

The deep human need for reciprocity is manifest not only in recreational gaming but in the ways people work and learn. Consider the so-called Hawthorne effect, discovered quite by accident by Elton Mayo in the course of his research on management effectiveness conducted in the late 1920s and early 1930s at Western Electric's Hawthorne plant on the outskirts of

Cicero, Illinois. Mayo speculated that a combination of sympathetic shop-floor management and improved working conditions would lead to an "undreamed era of active collaboration that will make possible an almost incredible human advance." Productivity went up when he turned up the lights, just as he had predicted. When he routinely turned the lights down again on his way to research another variable, productivity went up again — this time to his amazement. The lesson for management, conclude Peters and Waterman in *In Search of Excellence*, is that "it is attention to employees, not working conditions per se, that has the dominant impact on productivity."

Consider the story again, substituting "kids" for "workers" and "learning" for "productivity." Imagine an endless stream of educationally oriented Hawthorne-like effects, where the process of learning is made the more intense by the simple fact of attentive human contact. For it is not simply in terms of what children learn but how they learn that social interaction is important. Children blessed with attentive parents and the opportunity to learn in healthy social settings are more likely to learn how to put themselves in another's shoes than are the contact-deprived children of the Norwegian tundra. They are also likely to learn more effectively, and with greater pleasure, a broad range of skills.

We do ourselves no favors by attempting to depopulate the schools, to reduce the learning process to the intake of data stripped like a food pellet of all delicious character. It doesn't work; interest fades. Britain's highly successful televised Open University finds it necessary, as do other dispensers of televised education, to offer tutorials (with real tutors), periods of residency, and other devices to give the structure and human contact necessary to sustain motivation. Even if by some freak of nature people could gain a basic education in solitude, they would miss learning to get along and to take another's part.

Working It Out

Games are "buffered models of power contests," according to John Roberts and his colleague, Brian Sutton-Smith, which help to liberate the child from the trauma of helplessness at the same time they teach new attitudes and skills. Their "reconciliation" theory goes like this. Every culture induces in its children certain conflicts and anxieties — power discrepancies, for example, and conflicting desires to be fused and independent — through its child training procedures. These inevitably (and naturally) conflicted children are attracted to games which model their conflict by codifying its emotional and cognitive aspects and provide them, in the course of playing the game, an opportunity to develop confidence and competence to handle the real-life situations symbolized by the game. The game-playing is an exercise in sanctioned role reversals, a form of buffered learning about the operations of competitive and collaborative success — the cognitive, affective, and psychological; the interplay of chance, strategy, and physical skill — the full-scale practice of which is off-limits to children.

Games invite an exploration of feelings — screaming with fear at a terrible monster, roaring with rage at a "mother" or "father," imperiously directing an army of plastic soldiers, weeping in sorrow over the death of a "baby" — without the dangers that would be involved in exploring such feelings in real life. The game-player, it is said, can keep his character up and his costs down. The structure of the game and the understanding that it's just "pretend" are the safeguarding boundaries of this low-risk testing ground. Early childhood conflicts are assuaged, and the child makes step-by-step progress toward appropriate adult behavior.

Children learn to take the role of others, becoming differentially skilled participants in the business of face-to-face interaction. They learn how to assume, or avoid, the consequences of various sets of actions. Through games, children also learn the meaning of a rule, at once one of the key buffers between game-playing and the cold, cruel world, and a critical piece of grown-up learning.

Games are a sort of travelling puppet show which children, borrowing from inherited models, construct in their own backyard, framing the stage with found wood scraps, pulling socks over styrofoam spheres and pillowcases over heads. They renovate, reconstruct, and eventually demolish the thing, but while they play on a given stage they must follow the accompanying set of rules, for these rules define the fictional environment of the game. If they do not, the game does not function. There is no game.

Whether children play competitively or collaboratively is of no particular consequence here. What matters is that the rules be sufficiently fair to be agreeable to everyone concerned and the players be reasonably well-matched. Competition and collaboration are not polar opposites but inseparably interlocked, for a participant has to collaborate in order to compete, in games as in real life. If your opponent is not your match or not equipped with comparable resources, the contest is not considered fair and therefore isn't fun. If your opponent is exhausted of money or manpower or F111 fighter planes, there is no contest at all. Cheaters may violate the rules, but by cheating they are at least pretending to respect them, which is a form of obedience. It is obedience to the *idea* of rules. Only the nihilist can destroy the game, only one who denounces the rules as absurd and refuses to play because the game is meaningless. The nihilist's arguments are irrefutable because the game has none but intrinsic meaning.

Baseball Games

Games have their enculturative function — the subtle transmission of a culture's attitudes, values, and beliefs. Children also learn various social skills through game-playing, including how to take the role of others and how to deal acceptably with rules. The third general educational function of games (and we're still on games without deliberate educational intention) is the promotion of context-based skills. This function, like the others, extensively overlaps the other two. It is more a matter of emphasis than discrete attribute.

To play a game, children learn the numerous skills required to master and excel at that game — to hit a leather-covered ball with a smooth wooden bat, or a smaller, harder ball with the angled extension of an arm's length steel rod; to hide, to seek;

to calculate chess moves five deep and three wide. Like most people this side of schizophrenia, children respond to the situations in which they find themselves. "A child in a baseball game behaves baseball," observes Jerome Bruner in *Toward a Theory of Instruction.* He stands in a semi-squat with his hand on his knees, pushes his cap back to wipe his brow, and spits through his teeth. The fans are also contextually busy, computing averages and other indices of fate with such vigor that one could hypothesize that baseball is among Mother Nature's many clever ways to teach averaging. It seems to work, for although averaging is a subtle skill (a player's batting average changes faster at the beginning of a season than it does later on), some devotees, including many who have trouble with school math, develop an intuition for averaging that would amaze their despairing math instructors.

Of the context-based skills, those key to playing the game are the more identifiable. The peripheral skills such as averaging, mastery of which is more a spin-off than a direct result of game-playing, are harder to pin down as discrete outcomes and harder to predict. One is rarely certain in advance what peripheral skills will be gained by playing a particular game. They are therefore given less attention than the physical skills, strategic smarts and/or plain, ordinary luck that goes into getting the ball through the hoop or checking the king.

Both context-based and peripheral skill learning have educational potential if the game is so designed and the learning adequately supported. For the moment let us simply note that games offer a down-to-earth medium through which to transmit skills and ideas that might otherwise be incommunicable to children, either due to the complexity of the information or because the children are unprepared to receive it in abstract form. Games are dynamic models and like their static counterparts — model airplanes, architects' model buildings — they simplify reality to a level one can deal with, bringing it down (or up, like a two-foot double helix) to a scale one can handle, manipulate, study. If they are designed and supported with this intention, games can also bring the abstract to life by switching on its theoretical gears and letting it move into the realm of the concrete.

Learning with Intent

A game is an intentional learning game when the rules which govern its play demand the development and use of educationally valuable skills, the acquisition of important knowledge, or the exploration of a worthwhile facet of experience. Such games constitute a fundamentally different approach than that usually taken in schools, one based on the premise that children learn through guided, reciprocal interaction with their world — by acting, experiencing the consequences of their actions, and sharing their discoveries with others.

A series of acknowledgments has lead to the development of computer-based learning games and simulations, though not their wide use in schools. We have recognized that children are not learning much of what they need to know about our complex society. We have discovered that games, including those without educational intention, can be tremendously effective in teaching children about their culture, about getting along, winning, losing, and how (the list goes on) to hit a ball with a wooden bat. And we have found that the computer has much to offer as a games medium. While the computer has many limitations and cannot fulfill many of the traditional goals of non-computer games, it can increase the value of learning games by extending them into content-rich areas and enhancing the overall learning experience. We would do well to pursue the development of new learning games and simulations that approximate natural processes, applying the best methods and models from the old games to our current educational needs.

Among the potential virtues of games as intentional devices for learning are the same qualities found in "unintentional" games.

- They can be instrumental in shaping attitudes, values and beliefs, providing children simultaneously with information about their world and opportunities to practice changing it.

- Since they often involve two or more players, educational games extend the acquisition of formal learning into the informal realm. Even competitive games are collaborative, demanding regular, positive interaction between people. This reciprocal cooperation is one of the most powerful educational forces we know.

• Educational games can help students learn facts and skills integral, as well as peripheral, to the game. Players learn what they need to know in order to play the game, and this, if the game is well designed, can include educationally valuable information. Since the skills and information "have a place to go" within the fiction of the game, students are likely to retain that knowledge longer than they might by other means.

These positive attributes are not given wide credence, unverifiable as they are by the standard measures. Instead, games are subjected to the same harsh criteria with which we judge literature. Here's John Gardner, in *The Art of Fiction*:

> The business of education is to give the student both useful information and life-enhancing experience, one largely measurable, the other not; and since the life-enhancing value of a course in literature is difficult to measure — since, moreover, many people in a position to put pressure on educational programs have no real experience in or feeling for the arts — it is often tempting to treat life-enhancement courses as courses in useful information, putting them on the same "objective" level as courses in civics, geometry, or elementary physics. So it comes about that books are taught (officially, at least) not because they give joy, the incomparably rich experience we ask and expect of all true art, but because, as a curriculum committee might put it, they "illustrate major themes in American literature," or "present a clearly stated point of view and can thus serve as a vehicle for (certain) curriculum objectives ...." One cannot exactly say that such teaching is pernicious, but to treat great works of literature in this way seems a little like arguing for preservation of dolphins, whales, chimps, and gorillas solely on the grounds of ecological balance.

Since the educational system is increasingly inclined to dispense measured doses of objectively useful and testable information, and disinclined to leave room in the curriculum for life-enhancing experiences — experiences which, though lacking "proof," any sensitive observer would instantly and intuitively recognize as worthwhile — it tends also to look askance at learning games, to our great collective disadvantage.

Games are worthwhile for the simple sake of fun. If games can also stimulate interest in an educational activity, particularly one involving several children together, they are that much more valuable. While we do not have much hard evidence that children learn things deemed educationally useful directly from educational gaming, we can be sure that if they enjoy themselves while playing, their interest is likely to be greater than otherwise and therefore their probable time-on-task, which in turn has an impact on learning.

Common sense argues that games and simulations have more than fun to offer the intentional learning process. As intrinsically social, intrinsically collaborative activities, they convey the message that learning is a human activity, dependent on human interaction and involving shared understanding rather than adaptation to authority. (Another message, conveyed by the fun, is simply that learning is pleasurable.) This is particularly so if the computer is peripheral to the real action of the game and a catalyst for interactions among the players. If games have an appropriate mix of chance and skill, they provide opportunities for people of different abilities to learn together, in a manner which is fair and exciting for all. If they are so designed, they can explicitly (or implicitly) insist on interactions between players, demanding teamwork, distributed responsibilities, strategic collaboration, negotiation. And if they are so used in the classroom, they can provide valuable opportunities to reflect, after the play, on shared experiences and discoveries.

The Land of Aha!s Revisited

A simulation is a metaphor. The classroom becomes a metaphor of ancient Greece or the UN General Assembly; the closet and sun lamp become metaphors of night and day. The richness of the metaphor to a large extent determines the success of the simulation. If it is also well-designed and well-integrated with other methods of teaching, a simulation/learning game can take children on a wide-body magic carpet ride to the learning-intense Land of Aha!s, where learning is grounded in experience and vice versa.

A few brave, high-energy teachers may be able to provide *real* real projects, such as building a geodesic dome in the parking lot — projects which can bring the kids to Aha! That's great if one has the resources, but for most teachers it is too expensive, too labor- and space-intensive, and too likely to send a freckle-faced seventh grader to the hospital with a sprained back. It may be outright impossible to get there any other way but via computer simulations. Even if one can build domes and visit the UN, no one, by any method, can take a boat, plane, or slave-borne litter to a flat plane of the Peloponnesus in the year 418 BC. Computer simulations and learning games are the next best thing to being there. They're a manageable, low-risk alternative to a host of otherwise unattainable experiences. They're also cheap, relative to other methods, and not just because only one machine and one software program is required per classroom. Simulations can be used to achieve such marvels as a trip to the Peloponnesus not obtainable at any price.

Games and simulations can be fantastically exciting, thanks to the computer and its many roles, the best of which are invisible. The computer can maintain a large database, that stash of facts, figures, and interrelationships put there by the programmer to form the informational backbone of the game. Since a learning game simulates a real-life setting by mirroring many of the elements of that setting, and since the greater the number of variables reproduced the more the simulation feels like the real thing, the computer can create intensely vivid environments by drawing on its database for richer, more detailed variables. It thereby spares the teacher of this chore. She no longer has to simulate the Civil War by running around with a bandage on her head, although she still may choose to have the kids dress up in costume or decorate the room. Now she can devote herself to more valuable activities. The computer can also be programmed to use its storehouse of information in many different ways. A single game may be set to play at several levels of difficulty. Players may be able to change certain parameters — values, costs, and timers, for example — and thereby so alter the flavor of the game that it becomes quite a new game, with new challenges.

Computer simulations are, of course, not without limitations. A simulation may approach reality, but it is not reality and never can be. It should never be used if the real thing is available and viable as a learning experience under the conditions one is working. If you can go sailing, by all means do so. If you can translocate yourself and thirty kids to ancient Greece and back again, do it immediately. But if you settle for simulations because such field trips are out of range or impossible, be aware that much of the richness and color — the wind in your hair and salty sea spray in your face, the smells of cheese and sweat and dust, the bleating of the goats — cannot be simulated. Most of the variables cannot be known and if they were could not be included. Be aware that a simulation is loaded with judgments about what to include and what to leave out. These judgments, required of the designer by the constraints of the medium, shape the fine line between fact and fiction. Mistaken, they falsify the image. At minimum, they reflect, however subtly, a set of values which must be recognized as such by the teacher and in turn by the students.

But the limitations of the mode are at the same time its great strength. Since a simulation can never be as real as the real thing, the experience is open to the imagination of the players in the same way a book leaves the filling of textural gaps to the reader's imagination. The real/unreal duality leaves room for the player to press beyond the limits of reality, into the realm of what-might-be and back out again. Various kinds of training, from driver's education to orbital flight training, have long made use of the elastic quality of simulations. Fifteen-and-a-half years old, the dotted line racing toward the center of his brain, a boy can practice what to do when, at sixteen, he will be confronted with the Hazards of the Road. Likewise, astronauts would never have made it to the moon had it not been for skill-stretching, imagination-stretching flight simulations. Like these, the classroom simulations tolerate false theories, fanciful detours, and errors in judgment. It is precisely because one knows the experience is simulated that participation is attractive and stimulating.

Back in the future, students can explore the differences between what is real and what is conjured.

"How long did it take you to reach the New World?" the teacher might ask students who had just made the simulated voyage by sailing ship.

"Three days."

"How long did it take Columbus?"

"Three months."

Suddenly, Columbus' voyage becomes more vivid than it would have been if merely described as stretching from August 3 to October 12, 1492. With the help of a teacher, these differences can be the material for an entire learning experience, in addition to the primary one, based on the very fact that the simulated one was not real. The simulation's weakness has become a strength; the bug (as programmers are fond of saying) has become a feature.

Intentional games convey the notion, reminiscent of computer tools, that within their buffered environment it is safe to make mistakes. Mistakes are no longer mistakes but moves less desirable than others. Even major errors in judgment do not have catastrophic consequences. This is a double-edged attribute. Weizenbaum argues that video games are even more harmful than TV because they actively teach dissociation between what one does and the consequences of one's actions. One can blow up entire "planets" at the push of a button, suffering not the slightest twinge of guilt or sympathetic pain. Learning games must not include such seemingly inconsequential destruction, either as a goal or a gratuity. They can instead turn their low-risk quality to positive advantage by relieving children of the inhibiting dread of doing something wrong. Freed to explore and experiment within a world over which they have considerable control, children can learn, not in spite of seeing but *because* they see the consequences of their actions.

While the unreality of simulations is enticing, so is their local reality. Players temporarily induced to believe (or to agree not to disbelieve) that the experience is indeed real have an investment in the outcome. This investment is a powerful motivator. When one has something at stake, whether it's 25¢ at the video arcade or one's life savings at Belmont, one *cares*, and therefore one takes care to make the smartest possible moves. A couple of kids playing Energy Search, a simulation/game designed by Tom Snyder Productions, were overheard enthusing to their pals. "This is so cool," they said. "You get to make decisions that really count." Their decisions did not really count, of course — it's just a game — and at some level the kids knew that quite well. But it felt real enough during the game to make them want to make smart, careful moves.

Paying Attention to the Man behind the Curtain

How to achieve the powerful effects of a well-designed intentional learning game? It seems like fun, and it can be, but like other promising processes it is more difficult than one might think. The designer must strike a delicate balance between accessibility and challenge. The game can't be too simple, at the risk of being trivial, but neither can it be so complex as to be impenetrable by the willing learner. To do it well is so difficult and so expensive as to be beyond the reach of most classroom teachers working on their own. Neither do most publishers and development companies have the time, money, stamina, or expertise to design good learning games and simulations.

Let's take a look behind the scenes, at the process of game design and development. The process is interesting on its own merits, as was Saab's approach to car-making. It is also important that people know how games are made insofar as the process influences the final product. What is true for all educational software is especially true with games. We entrust ourselves and our children, however briefly, to the care and influence of the software and thereby to the creator of that software. "When you play a video game," writes Turkle, "you enter the world of the programmers who made it." Behind the sightless, impassive screen is a guy, just a guy, not an omniscient other. His personality comes through — his quirks, values, and sense of humor, and the process by which he works. We should know this when we look for new games and agree to enter their powerful worlds. It is a distinctly intimate relationship.

The Indivisible Medium

What does it take to make a good game? It takes programming skill, subject matter expertise, and knowledge both of how to teach and how children learn, which are not necessarily the same thing. It also takes intense concentration, a vision of the end product as clear and unconfused as a Mozart flute concerto, and a willingness to make the kind of commitment and sacrifice usually associated with artistic endeavor.

There are plenty of good teachers in this world, plenty of computer wizards, inventors of games, subject matter experts, and obsessive, driven workers, but it is a rare person who combines all their attributes and is still able to walk in a straight line. When such a person is found, he or she must then be managed, which is in itself a tall order. Artists — and game designers are software artists — are notoriously unmanageable, and when that factor is compounded with the notorious unpredictablility of software projects, the situation becomes so wooly that managers rush to find alternatives.

Hence the tendency of publishers to use committees, with agenda and specifications they can pass on down the hierarchy to arrive at the jerry-built stuff that passes for educational software. They do this not only out of economic necessity but under a mistaken belief in the divisibility of the medium.

A computer game looks as if it has handles to grab hold of and places to sit down. The uninitiated may conclude that it is therefore divisible into manageable units, each of which can be designed quickly and to spec by a subcommittee, then joined to the other units. "Because the medium is tractable," writes Frederick Brooks, "we expect few difficulties in implementation; hence our pervasive optimism."

The group starts out with a set of learning objectives or license to use a children's book as the basis for their game. An in-house developmental psychologist identifies the possibility of teaching A, B, and C skills and meeting X, Y, and Z objectives. Additional input from educational experts, software engineers and designers is pulled together into one very tight, very detailed specification which in turn is handed to programmers to implement. Implementers are coding slaves, at the bottom of the heap.

This approach is disastrous, as we saw with CAI. Committees are famous for stifling initiative and creativity, and educational software committees are no exception. All the experts in the world can't guarantee a good program any more than they can a good children's book. They shoot down new ideas because they're new, not bad, and therefore are threatening on some level, if only because they require attention. Alternatively, the committee gives a project so much attention it withers under "analysis paralysis." Whatever the project or the configuration of the group, there is never any shortage of reasons why *not* to do something. Harvard's John Steinbrunner put it this way in *The Cybernetic Theory of Decision*: "It is inherently easier to develop a negative argument than to advance a constructive one."

The Hemlock Chair

Writing about the management problems afflicting large programming projects, Brooks points out that "workers and units of time are interchangeable only when a task can be partitioned among many workers with no communication among them." The design and development of a good learning game is essentially an unpartitionable task, as all the elements must be fused into a single, seamless whole. The task also involves complex interrelationships between the people working on it. The more people on the committee, the more difficult it is to avoid misunderstandings and miscommunication, especially where each member has a different area of expertise. Some may not understand the educational thrust of the game, and others may not understand what the medium can and cannot do.

Let's say that Denise, Rob, and Joan set about to design a wooden chair (on paper; none of them knows Thing One about wood except that it grows on trees). They call for a dramatic, sweeping back with pencil-thin spindles and armrests which echo the curve of the back. They want the legs to be slender but not skinny, making it look as if the chair were floating, and for personal reasons too obtuse to explain, they want it made of hemlock. But when they hand the specs to a carpenter, he tells them that, much to his regret, the wood they have chosen will snap into a hundred little pieces if forced into the specified shape. "Surely you can do it," insist Joan, Rob, and Denise. "We have it all figured out." "Nope," says the carpenter. "Won't work that way." Likewise, our educational game committee may come up with a host of marvelous and indisputably educational features that, alas, would eat up 255K of memory and push the little game up to fourteen diskettes. Someone down the line has to say, "Nope, it won't work that way."

How to manage the entire design process in such a way as to produce the best, most invigorating, challenging and fun games on the education market? The two (or three or four) specialites represented must each move closer together, like the members of the Saab-making teams who, in taking a turn at each task, got a sense of the whole. The chair committee needs to learn about wood, to understand the flow of the grain and the nuances of the texture, and the carpenter must learn more about the kind of chair the committee really wants. So, too, must friendly and productive relationships be formed between the teachers who use the software and the designers and programmers who create it. It is not sufficient that educators be used merely as focus groupies and advisors. Their involvement must be more fundamental. Educators should visit development areas and learn more about the technology of which they are making such demands. And the programmer must find ways to keep in constant touch with the educational realm, with the issues, the educators, and the children.

Going It Alone

To preserve its artistic and conceptual integrity, a good game or simulation must ultimately be designed, and programmed, by one person alone. Some delegation may make sense on data-intensive projects with a lot of graphics or text that could be plugged in later, but for most software of any kind one person must be in charge. Lotus 1-2-3 is the most successful business software on the market. Written by Jonathan Sachs, working alone for months in a little cubicle in Littleton, Massachusetts, it is a far better program than its grandiose cousin, Symphony, which was written by a team. The personal toll on Sachs was terrible, as it is for anyone who undertakes such a project. (Eight, ten, twelve hours a day of superhuman concentration of a sort most mortals can stand for only three hours. Family and friends sacrificed like rabbits on the highway.)

Who can do the job of educational game development? A rare person. Call him Seth. In previous lives he may have been a philosophy major, a French minor, a short-order cook, an MBA, a dental hygienist, a horticulturalist, or a second story man, but now he works around the clock in a room thick with positive ions and mental energy. Contrary to popular opinion, which perversely insists that unlike other workers, all programmers are aggressively indifferent to creature comforts and personal hygiene, Seth prefers a nice room with windows. If his running shoes look like toxic waste, well, they're not his only pair. Seth looks tired yet ferociously awake. He also looks so very anxious one might think he just learned he has cancer if it weren't for the intermittent sparkle in his eye.

The man is driven by the anxiety peculiar to those with total responsibility for an enormous artistic project. It's as if he were building a Saab all the way up from the pistons and the crankcase to a baby blue custom pinstripe, only more so. His medium offers a near-infinite range of choices — about color and shape, plot, character, and dialogue — at the same time it demands absolute conformity. It may be earth, air, fire, and water, but not one semicolon can be out of place or the magic doesn't work. Since his job is not readily subject to partitioning, Seth must work as hard and as fast as he can, like a one-armed paperhanger whose glue-slathered paper will return to its familiar curl if he does not smooth it quickly on the wall. He does it for a million reasons, some of them doubtless pathological but including a passionate sense of artistic ownership. He is literally an owner in that he'll share in the royalties if his game sells. He is also an artist fired with the certainty that no one else on the face of the earth could design a game just like his.

Our programmer cannot be separated from the designer without damage to the product. Any attempt to do so, such as a team approach in which a list of specs is handed to implementers, fails to acknowledge the instincts and the influence of the programmer. The programmer has nine-tenths of the power anyway, so he might as well have all of it. Consider the difference between building software and building a building. If you're a structural engineer working with an architect's specs, you have to follow those specs. There is a limit on your creativity. If you suddenly discover that the ground won't hold up under the proposed design, you have to go back to the architect and say, "Uh, we have a problem." Not so with software development. The programmer is quite alone when at 2 AM, he discovers that the ground won't hold up under the design, so he fixes the problem himself. He has to be expected to be creative.

Designer/programmers like Seth have such great responsibility, and their influence on educational games so strong, that they must be people who not only can do the work but can make the games interesting for kids. They must be interesting people, appealing, energetic, like good teachers everywhere.

The Great American Computer Game

The approach to game design at Tom Snyder Productions is an artistic one, not formulaic. The designer/programmer envisions a consistent environment where the concepts she wants to work with really matter, an environment worth exploring. She does not attach a bogus game to a set of skills in the vain hope that kids won't notice they're being had. Instead, she develops an environment that will appeal to kids, with an intriguing predicament. A sailing ship one must navigate across the ocean in a race for the wealth of the New World; a search for the kidnapper of Lily the dolphin, in the suspect-riddled town of Costa Villa; the challenge of Metallica and Darksome Mire — these are examples of enticing situations that kids like to explore and that keep them involved in learning. The games and the skills flow naturally from here.

With the game environment established, however loosely, the designer has a base on which to begin building a learning game. Soon she will disappear into her room, but she still has some important work to do with her colleagues and her manager. They will help her focus on the audience, encourage her to keep the player in mind and to remember what turns kids on.

How to imagine kids' reaction to a game? One good way is to plan for the dialogue one would like to hear if eavesdropping on a couple of game-playing kids. Manager and programmer take this step together, and in doing so they engage in a form of interaction that is more likely to be transmitted to the game-playing experience than if the game were designed by one person alone. This partnership is a strong device. The partners can encourage and stimulate one another's imagination in a dynamic yet manageable way at the same time they build into the design process the reciprocity that is so important to learning. The method, observes Olds in "Sometimes Children Are the Best Teachers," is also in synch with what good teachers know intuitively;

> that learning will occur if you can get students involved in a discussion, where they start to ask the right kind of questions and struggle to formulate answers that can be understood by someone else.

Imagine what you'd like to overhear from two kids learning about U.S. geography. As you pass Marcie's room on the way to the kitchen, you hear her say to Elaine, "How did we get from Dallas to Hartford so quickly the last time?" You might not be able to put your finger on why, exactly, but your intuition will tell you that Elaine and Marcie are learning something worthwhile. That fragment of dialogue would have been typical of the quotes assembled long before the game took shape by the creators of Agent USA, a TSP geography game.

Let's say one wanted to develop a program about the solar system. Instead of grappling with a set of educational specifications, the manager-programmer team might approach the problem differently, by putting together a list of quotes they'd like to hear. This approach leads to software which begs to be played by a group of two or more.

> *"How fast can you get us to Mercury?"* ("You" indicates task-differentiated teamwork and a sense that the players have active control over their movements. If the children were forced to depend solely on the computer for their travel arrangements, they might say something more passive, such as "How fast can we get to Mercury?")

> *"Hand me the star map."* (Since not all necessary infor-
> mation is provided by the computer, the kids must turn
> to outside sources.)
>
> *"Wait a second! Does that star belong in Scorpio?"* (The kids
> are learning the constellations, and distinguishing be-
> tween planets and stars.)
>
> *"Rats! Why do we have to run low on fuel right at the edge
> of the Milky Way?"* (Tension is high. Investment level is
> high.)
>
> *"Do you hear that!?"* (Accompanied by ominous sounds
> from the computer. The kids are alert to every quirk
> and wrinkle in the environment of the game. They are
> watching, waiting, for the tiniest something that will
> either trip them up — kids love to be randomly con-
> founded — or give them a clue to the best strategy.)

This dialogue breathes life into the imaginary environment.
The designer/programmer takes it the next logical step by writing a short story rich in dialogue, almost like a play. Just as a
story can help kids remember that certain frogs have blue hair,
the act of committing the story to paper forces the designer to
be consistent in her organization of the game while giving her
places to put all the pesky little details. It is responsive yet
technologically undemanding, while the computer tends at this
stage to be limiting. The programmer can work with paper and
pencil, with file folders sorted like chapters in a book, each one
chock-full of questions and ideas, character sketches and frag-
ments of dialogue. The story also gives her something to discuss
with her colleagues, something they can applaud or augment
or say about, "That's terrible!"

What happens next? Blood. Sweat. Tears. And magic-making
by the person who alone has the job of developing a learning
game. Once the game is written — and it must be a powerful,
exciting, absorbing, unique, authentic game — kids are brought
in to play it. Playtesting at TSP is an informal activity. The
playtesting director is more of an equipment manager than
adult supervisor. He plays with the kids, takes note of their
excitement and interactions, their questions and the skills they
seem to learn, and feeds his observations to the game designer.

The designer then rushes in to build additional supports for the skills conveyed by the game. Above all, she uses what works and what makes learning come naturally.

Are We There Yet?

Outside the inner sanctum, in the rough-and-tumble world between the classroom and the computer store, how is one to distinguish between a terrible game and a good one?

A good learning game or simulation, unlike many popular games, *helps the learner to learn*. Consider the popular board game, *Scrabble*, which asks that players piece together words from randomly selected letters and connect those words on the game board in crossword-puzzle fashion. The more extensive one's vocabulary and the better one is able to decipher words from a hodge-podge of scrambled letters, the better one will do at the game, but the vocabulary and the spelling skills must be developed away from the game. *Scrabble* does not afford the inexperienced or ignorant player an opportunity to learn, even to refer to outside references such as dictionaries or knowledgeable friends. The game, like some archaic form of CAI, is a test of what is already known rather than a context for gathering new information. So is a spelling bee, which, although it may motivate students to prepare for public competition, does not in itself include the learning activity. In neither game is the educationally valuable content — knowledge of words and how to spell them — something that one is helped to learn by playing the game.

Contrast this with two computer learning games created by Tom Snyder Productions. In Agent USA, the player's challenge is to stop the FuzzBomb (a TV set gone bad) threatening to turn the entire country into helpless FuzzBodies. The game does not test knowledge, but instead encourages children to learn while playing the game. Kids learn the capitols of the forty-eight contiguous states and their general location, not because that information is taught directly but because in only the capitol cities are there InfoBooths with maps detailing the spread of the Fuzz, the location of the FuzzBombs, and the crystal strength (the antidote) in each city. The player can freeze the game at will, taking as much time as he wishes to study the maps, computer and non-computer, and other pertinent information without interfering with the play of the game. Here the computer is not the unrelenting force it is in so many games (and virtually all CAI programs). It is more like a gracious host, providing both the inducement and the opportunity to learn in an exciting, though not hysterical, atmosphere, laced, at the player's choice, with calm.

SpellDiver is a spelling and vocabulary game. Once upon a time a young space traveller named Gabdoc came to earth. Gabdoc wrote long homesick notes to its mama by carving huge words in the ground — words so big they could be read, by special instrument, all the way from Gabdoc's home planet. Over the centuries the movement of the earth displaced some of the words from each note and shifted them to the bottom of the ocean. The goal of SpellDiver is to uncover the words, now encrusted with a seeweed-like growth called lettermoss, and place them in their proper places in Gabdoc's notes home. The player controls a diver, named Oshianna Jones, who has a five-minute air tank with which to do the job. Additional air can be purchased, but at great expense. By moving Oshianna Jones over the lettermoss, the player exposes what is underneath to a wide-scan sonar device above water. The player can refer to the sonar readings at any time to get a wider view of the fragmentary letters as they come together into words. The game is frozen during that period. The game also includes a do-it-yourself option, which allows a teacher or friend to put new words into the program.

Like Agent USA, SpellDiver does not test knowledge but encourages its acquisition. Most players need to uncover only a few letters before they can complete a given word. Without prompting, while the game is frozen, they enthusiastically seek out a dictionary or knowledgeable friend to narrow their choices among likely words and confirm the spelling of the words they choose. They discover new words and learn how to spell, all in the active course of the game.

Human-assisted Instruction

A good learning game or simulation *fosters the kind of interactive play appropriate to what is being learned.* Most computer games, educational and otherwise, are designed for just one player. Some have two kids playing against each other, usually with joysticks and a split screen. But the same two (or more) kids could form a team and play against the computer. One computer could be used to take an entire class on an in-house field trip to a simulated New World. Or two teams, each with its own computer and separated potentially by thousands of miles, could compete/collaborate with each other via modem-linked telephone lines. The range of possible interactive styles is widening under the impetus of hardware invention. Let us also consider these styles in the low-tech light of educational content.

Geography Search simulates the fifteenth-century voyage of several ships from the fictional land of Vesuvia, racing across the ocean to find wealth in the New World. Clearly, the metaphor's real-world parallel is unavailable. The game requires that each crew of four to five players successfully pilot its ship's course based on information supplied and managed by the computer. If one crew decides to sail due west for half a day, the computer provides them with information similar to what would have been available to real fifteenth-century sailors, to be used to plot the course and decide the next action. It supplies pictures of the stars as would be seen from a ship in that position, from which the crew members decipher latitude; the sun's shadow and a clock (longitude); wind direction and wind speed (based on trade winds); the angle a ship of its type can sail with the given wind; ocean depth (given the distance from the coast and known underwater mountain ranges); and clouds and storms (both functions of location).

The computer does this with a speed and efficiency no person can match, relieving the players and the teacher of that labor while creating an extraordinarily rich environment, and it does it in such a way as to encourage productive interactions among the players' both on and away from the computer. The relevant information for each sailing crew is flashed on a "Quick Screen" for only a few moments, too short a time for any one person to gather it all. (The device can be shut off when teams have fewer than three members.) Within a few turns — and again, without prompting — most groups will divide the responsibility for gathering information in the different categories. Each member of the crew, no matter how shy or "slow," becomes an indispensible specialist in at least one area since his or her information is as vital as the next guy's to the collective fate of the team. Once the data is plucked from the screen, crew members move away from the machine to share their findings and together make a decision about the next move.

In Bannercatch, a computer simulation of Capture the Flag, player interaction is intrinsic to the game in a very different way. Instead of two players competing against each other, they collaborate in devising and carrying out a strategy to defeat the computer (alias Max and his wily band of robots). The two players are a team, and as such they must negotiate their roles and responsibilities — guarding their own flag, attacking the robot flag, releasing humanoid teammates from jail. Children often decide to balance their involvement by taking turns attacking and defending. As the robot strategies become increasingly fierce through progressively difficult levels of play, the human players must cooperate all the more.

The Other Side offers still another example of positive, built-in inter-human interaction. This simulation game about global conflict resolution is set in a generic world of limited resources in which two nations (one side and the other side) must work toward a common goal, the building of a unifying bridge, while each maintains its own economy. The game can be played competitively or collaboratively, but in either mode, communication with the other side is limited to a short-fused computer Hotline. Misunderstandings inevitably arise, and CAD, the aggressive Computer Assisted Defense system, can escalate those misunderstandings into real conflict. Played either with one or two computers, The Other Side demonstrates the difficulties of dealing with another person, group, or nation whose motives are not entirely clear.

The educational intention of the game is to promote the learning of strategies of peace. Players on each team must organize themselves to collect information from a version of the Quick Screen, and must work together to balance short- and long-term goals, formulate defensive and offensive strategies, interpret Hotline messages from the other side, and compose their own messages to send. The interdependency of teammates is extensive, as is each team's dependency on the other, for neither side has sufficient resources to build the bridge by itself. One team cannot win by defeating the other. The graphics are designed to reinforce this message. Rewards are associated with building the bridge, while dropping a bomb, either as a hostile act or to release underground fuel reserves, evokes no vivid fireworks, merely the silent removal of objects from the world. If players contaminate the world through wanton bomb dropping, the computer abruptly terminates the game.

In its own oblique way, the Computer Assisted Defense system helps players accept the complex challenge of peace. CAD is above all a self-preservation mechanism with no interest in building the bridge, only in protecting its country. Its decisive countermeasures under threat are sometimes destructive to the delicate balance of world power and always illustrative of the fact that things do not always go as planned. Its hardline behavior keeps players on their toes, and demands that they take a high level of responsibility for their actions, both international and domestic. Representing a generic conglomeration of political and economic forces, including those the nation's leadership doesn't agree with and whose behavior it can't control, CAD may act contrary to the team's plans. Yet teammates, as ambassadors for their entire nation, must take responsibility for CAD's actions in their dealings with the other side. CAD also demands that each team employ a foreign policy not detrimental to its country's well-being. It won't allow one side to give its resources to the other in order for that side to build the bridge alone.

All for One and One for All

A good learning game has its educational content so well integrated with the playing that *learning how to play and improving game performance lead naturally to substantive learning.* Of the game's numerous interlocking elements, all have educational import. No one segment bears too much of the instructional burden, and none are merely decorative.

Learning by way of these well-integrated games can encompass many lessons at a time — lessons about specific subjects, including tool use, and human behavior. With The Other Side, students learn the effective use of social skills — teamwork, cooperation, negotiation, compromise, communication. They also gain a rare appreciation for the complexity of international relations in a world like our own, of limited resources, common and conflicting goals, and pervasive ambiguity. Any number of the many facets of the learning experience may capture their interest — conflict resolution on the global, national, and personal levels; interaction with the microcomputer as a communications conduit; interaction with classmates, incuding teammates and the invisible ones on the other side; risk-analysis; mapping, record-keeping and note-taking; strategic decision making. Any and all of these lessons have educational merit.

In Run For The Money, two players learn a collection of business skills, including the use of a computerized financial spreadsheet. Each player controls a Bizling, an interplanetary entrepreneur who has crash-landed on the planet Simian. In order to finance the getaway, each Bizling goes into business on Simian, buying raw materials called "rufs," converting the rufs into synthetic bananas ("synanas"), and selling the synanas to Simian's monkey inhabitants. Players make use of What If machines to explore the interconnections between the various aspects of their business, including the price of synanas, units sold, number of rufs purchased, cost per ruf, and advertising cost. Changes in these variables affects profit and hence the Bizling's chances of getting away. A monetary award is given to players who use the What If machine to accurately predict their profit for each period of buying and selling.

Run For The Money is playable at both ends of the competition/collaboration spectrum. The two players can compete with one another in the production, pricing, and purchase of equipment needed to repair their ships — the goal being a successful launch from Simian — or they can cooperate to insure that they both are able to launch at the same time. No reward is given to the first to leave. Whichever strategy is chosen, the process of choosing involves extensive social interplay. In one case a mixed strategy emerged after an initially competitive approach created a large capital discrepancy between the players. The game would have been an easy win for one player and a slow loss for the other. With a little pleading, the losing player convinced the other to make some pricing changes in order to keep him in the game. Subsequently, the two determined prices jointly while continuing to compete for equipment for their spaceships.

The computer game can also promote the use of non-computer tools. SpellDiver facilitates use of the dictionary. Geography Search supports mapmaking. And Agent USA fosters the use of a map without prompting or directives. The player in the role of Agent USA must travel by railroad around the country, dropping and harvesting special crystals in an effort to stem the spread of Fuzz from city to city. A system of local and rocket trains connects the forty-eight state capitols and the fifty-two other largest cities in the continental United States. The game package includes train schedules and a map for players to use in plotting a course to intercept the FuzzBomb responsible for the spreading Fuzz. Advanced players with an extensive knowledge of geography may be able to get by without the map, but others turn to it as an essential tool, freezing the game while they do so. As they become increasingly familiar with the location of the states and capitols — that information being an integral part of the game — players tend to convert the tangible tool into a conceptual one, relying more on the map in their heads than the one included with the game.

The History of Baseball

A good learning game *makes learning accessible* by building on understandings and patterns of knowledge already in place. It is a form of participatory fiction, and like all good fiction it is appealing and intriguing and encouraging of exploration. Like any good game, it draws from the culture, from rituals connected, however tangentially, with the values and practices of one's people.

The boy "behaving baseball" was following rituals perhaps 300 years old, rituals resonant, whether he knows it or not, with the broad consciousness of his culture. Abner Doubleday was said to have invented the game in Cooperstown, New York in

1839. Others claim that baseball derives from rounders, a game played in England as early as the 1600s and involving hitting a ball with a bat and advancing around bases. Although in 1906 a major league commission to investigate the so-called Doubleday Theory concluded, on the strength of a letter from a boyhood friend, that Doubleday indeed was the inventor, historical evidence now points to rounders as the original form. The game was modified over the years, and standardized, and now we have baseball, that quintessentially American game of warm-blooded chess, of lone heroes beating the odds on grassy fields just barely tame. Writes Barzun, "Whoever wants to know the heart and mind of America had better learn baseball."

All games are models of some sort, as we have seen. Baseball happens to be a hybrid of physical skill and strategy, and it happens that children learn, through playing it, physical and strategic skills, skills associated with teamwork and, as a spin-off, some mental arithmetic. Intentional educational games can derive tremendous strength from a grounding in familiar models like baseball, for they help children approach learning by already well-travelled routes. They have that quality the psychologists call "representativeness," by tapping into the intense imagination of children involved in a good story, a story children long to enter and do, in fantasy. A little boy named Michael went so far as to try to climb inside a book. "Unwilling to believe that so wonderful a world was unreachable," writes Michael's friend Carol Sternhell in an article in the *New York Times Book Review*, "he simply opened the tale to his favorite page, carefully arranged his choice on the floor and stepped in. He tried again and again, certain he would soon get it right, and each time he was left standing out in the cold he cried in bewilderment." Kids put a blanket over a cardtable, crawl inside with a plate of cookies, and suddenly they're in a pirate's hideaway surrounded by gleaming jewels. The stories they've heard of buried treasure, of one-eyed pirates gripping sabers in their teeth, lend the vivid, authenticating detail that helps children enter the dream-world of fiction.

Educational games open the door to experiences one can enter, as one enters the world inside a book or plays a centuries-old recreational game — experiences charged with the powerful excitement of kids hiding under a blanket-draped cardtable and made all the more powerful by building on concepts resonant with the culture. Computers open the door still wider by letting children participate in ways unattainable by young Michael's method or by any other means. The medium is as familar to them now as were baseball gloves and dollhouses to their parents.

Geography Search makes accessible an experience children have heard about and sung about but have never been able to enter as active participants. It resonates way back to the Niña and the Pinta and that discovery of America. Agent USA (the menace, the chase) feels like a cross between Superman, a spy thriller, and cops and robbers. Kids "ride" archetypical trains that go chunka-chunka-chunk, and they make use of the traditional travellers' aids, the map and the train schedule. These objects, like the maps, captain's logs, and record-keeping charts that come with Geography Search, link the world of the game to the palpable real world. The games are all the more resonant for straddling the two. Run For The Money links fantasy and the business world, a shorter leap, perhaps, if only in the time dimension. Players use real tools including graphs, surveys, and accounting spreadsheets, just like the folks in Houston and Silicon Valley.

In all of these games, the computer is necessary but not sufficient for learning. The class, not the computer, is the center of attention. When you walk into a good classroom simulation, you should see lots of action but have trouble finding the computer. Geography Search, for example, uses the computer in a way that addresses the realities of scarce computer resources and thirty kids per class. One computer is enough for all those kids. Rather than locking into each one of them individually, the computer helps to promote invigorating, instructive, reinforcing group dynamics. By allowing kids to find ways to encourage and challenge each other, it provides temporary relief from the problem of teachers addressing themselves too much to everyone and not enough to any one child. It demands no special computer training for students or teachers, relying instead on methods already familiar to both — small group activity, use of workbooks, pencils, paper.

This is a function of design — the deliberate promotion of regular, positive interaction between people and their environment. One method is to require the use of peripheral materials such as the maps and charts as well as resource materials usually found in abundance in the classroom. Nowhere does it say, "Talk this over with your teammates," but the need for doing so is compelling. Nowhere does it say, "Get a pencil and paper"; the kids just start playing and phone numbers start coming up and stray bits of information, and the kids think, "I'll remember that." But before long they're calling out, "Pencil! I need a pencil!" They start writing things down, happily, excitedly, because they have reason to do so. In a good game or simulation, children are free to use peripheral materials, and to interact positively with their peers and teachers, without penalty and without fear of losing their place.

Easy Pieces

> The music teacher held up the egg yolk-yellow cover of Beethoven's *Easy Compositions for the Piano.* "Remember this," she said with a frown, her Austrian accent reinforcing the words' severity. "There are no easy pieces."

Learning games and simulations do not teach any more than do other forms of educational software. The difference is that they can help to create environments where children learn and teachers teach. This magnificent opportunity carries with it a comparable challenge, for games are also not immune from the management problems shared by other software. One kid playing Agent USA in the corner of the classroom is no easier to handle than a kid doing CAI in the opposite corner.

The problem is not an easy one to solve. Very few simulations are designed expressly for the classroom, with its thirty kids under the tutelage of a teacher herself under the cloud of too many curriculum requirements and too little time. A few are so designed, yet even those are not for the generic classroom. They cannot be plopped into the middle of a class and expected to make immediate sense, nor can they be prescribed across the board as a standard part of a curriculum. The best classroom software money can buy is less generically ready for that class than any textbook or field trip one can imagine.

Textbooks, by wide consensus, are manageable. Their delivery system, which consists of setting the thing on the desk and opening to page one, is understood by every teacher in the country and nearly every child. Textbooks also have built-in highs and lows — built-in opportunities on the high end for teachers to take the material and run, and on the low end, a fail-safe mechanism whereby, if the teacher is absent or short on skills, the learners can still do all right on their own in learning about the subject of the textbook.

Software is different. Simulations and learning games have a slight advantage over LOGO and the non-specific, "thinking skills" software in that simulations are imbedded in identifiable content areas and therefore can be appropriately positioned (and sometimes justified) within the curriculum. But placement is the least of problems. What about nuts and bolts delivery? What about booting up and getting the thing running and the kids at the software equivalent of page one? Unlike with textbooks, the kids are lost without the teacher when it comes to running most classroom simulations. If the teacher lacks the skills and enthusiasm needed to make use of a simulation, the kids are likely to get less from the experience than they would watching TV. If the teacher is absent, they get nothing.

Simulations and games can be made easier to use on a practical, technological level. With the files coherent, the menus consistent, and the bugs eradicated, most educational games would be "friendlier" than they are at present. Still, we're so far away from the ease we take as commonplace with textbooks that it is almost foolhardy to talk at this time about making simulations comparably easy to use. Moreover, just as there are two kinds of interactivity, there are two kinds of ease of use, and the second one is the real kicker. The harder developers work to make simulations rich enough to be worthwhile, with exciting things going on in the program and between the players, the harder they are going to be *pedagogically* to use. Why? Because simulations beg for intense teacher involvement, and the better the simulation, the greater the requisite involvement.

There is no getting around the conflict between increasingly rich simulations and teachers' willingness to tolerate the attendant ambiguity and interactivity. Teacher training may help, but what we're dealing with here is something which, although it can be learned, cannot be readily taught. Experience may help, and models of simulations may be effectively conducted, but this too is not enough. Fact is, there are no easy pieces, and no short cuts to good teaching. A well-designed game or simulation sparks teachable moments, where kids will ask, "Hey, how do I figure out where I am from the stars?" or, "If the wind is blowing from the west, am I north or south of the equator?"

The teacher can respond directly, but he doesn't have to. The books, charts, maps, and other students will often suffice to answer children's questions. This takes patience and the wisdom to resist the impulse to help too soon. It also requires the kind of subtle control of the classroom achieved only by good teachers. As always, they must be the chief motivator, mixing practice with conceptual advances and making learning come alive and come naturally. Games and simulations are not the only useful software on the path to the most amazing thing. They have many weaknesses, including the grim facts that they cannot teach and are not easy to use, but those are failings shared by all forms of computerized education. Their worth lies in taking kids, with the skillful, sensitive help of a teacher, on a guided in-house field trip to the zoo or to the moon.

BIBLIOGRAPHY

Agee, Roy. "Are We Really Training Computer Teachers?" *T.H.E. Journal*, March 1985.

Avedon, Elliot M., and Brian Sutton-Smith (eds.). *The Study of Games*. New York: John Wiley and Sons, Inc., 1978.

Barzun, Jacques. "Scholarship Versus Culture." *Atlantic Monthly*, November 1984.

————. Quoted by Joseph L. Reichler in "Baseball" entry in *The World Book Encyclopedia*, 1975.

Bates, John A. "Extrinsic Reward and Intrinsic Motivation: A Review with Implications for the Classroom." *Review of Educational Research*, v. 49, no. 4, 1979.

Becker, Henry Jay. *School Uses of Microcomputers: Reports from a National Survey*. Center for Social Organization of Schools, Baltimore, Maryland: The Johns Hopkins University, v. 1–6, April 1983–November 1984.

Berman, Paul, and Milbry Wallin McLaughlin. "Implementing and Sustaining Motivations." *Federal Programs Supporting Education Change*, v. 3: Santa Monica, CA: The Rand Corporation, 1978.

Bok, Derek. "The President's Report, 1983–84." Cambridge: Harvard University, March 1985.

Bork, Alfred. "Education and Computers: The Situation Today and Some Possible Futures." *T.H.E. Journal*, October 1984.

Brooks, Frederick P., Jr. *The Mythical Man-Month: Essays on Software Engineering*. Reading, MA: Addison-Wesley Publishing Company, 1975.

Bruner, Jerome. *Toward a Theory of Instruction*. Cambridge: Harvard University Press, 1966.

————. *The Process of Education*. Cambridge: Harvard University Press, 1960.

Bruner, Jerome, Alison Jolly, and Kathy Sylva (eds.). *Play—Its Role in Development and Evolution*. New York: Basic Books, 1976.

Clements, Douglas H. "Logo Programming: Can It Change How Children Think?" *Electronic Learning*, January 1985.

Coburn, Peter, Peter Kelman, Nancy Roberts, Thomas F. F. Snyder, Daniel H. Watt, and Cheryl Weiner. *Practical Guide to Computers in Education*. Reading, MA: Addison-Wesley, 1982.

Deken, Joseph. *The Electronic Cottage*. New York: Bantam Books, 1983. (Originally published by Morrow, in 1981.)

Denzin, Norman. *Childhood Socialization*. Washington, D.C.: Jossey-Bass Publishers, 1977.

Dockterman, David A. "The Role of Educational Computer Games in Informal Learning Environments." Photocopied. Cambridge: Harvard University, May 1984.

————. "Computers and Education: Issues in Curriculum Change." Photocopied. Cambridge: Harvard University, January 1983.

Elkin, David. *Child Development and Education: A Piagetian Perspective.* New York: Oxford University Press, 1976.

Evaluation of Educational Software: A Guide to Guides. Edited by Nancy Baker Jones and Larry Vaughan. Chelmsford: Northeast Regional Exchange, Inc., and Austin: Southwest Educational Development Laboratory, 1983.

Family Guide to Educational Software. Topeka: The L. F. Garlinghouse Company, Inc. Winter 1984.

Friedrich, Otto. "The Computer Moves In." *Time*, 3 January 1983.

Frude, Neil. *The Intimate Machine: Close Encounters with Computers and Robots.* New York: New American Library, 1983.

Gardner, John. *The Art of Fiction: Notes on Craft for Young Writers.* New York: Random House, 1985. (Originally published by Knopf, 1983.)

Garvey, Catherine. *Play.* Cambridge: Harvard University Press, 1977.

Geiser, Kenneth, and Bennett Harrison. "The High-Tech Industry Comes Down to Earth." *Boston Globe*, 23 June 1985.

Gordon, Horace G., David Roberts, and Michael N. Milone, Jr. "Ten Myths About Microcomputers." *Academic Therapy* v. 19, no. 3, January 1984.

Hanson, Dirk. *The New Alchemists: Silicon Valley and the Microelectronics Revolution.* New York: Avon Books, 1982.

Herndon, James. *How to Survive in Your Native Land.* New York: Simon and Schuster, 1971.

Hollos, M. and P. A. Cowan. "Social Isolation and Cognitive Development: Logical Operations and Role-taking Abilities in Three Norwegian Settings." *Child Development*, v. 44, 1973. Quoted by Sluckin, 1981.

Holt, John. Quoted in "Education at Home: A Showdown in Texas." *Newsweek*, 25 March 1985.

———. *How Children Fail.* Revised edition, New York: Delacorte Press/Seymour Lawrence, 1982.

Hood, John F. and the Staff of the Curriculum Information Center, a division of Market Data Retrieval. "Microcomputers in Schools, 1984–85: A Comprehensive Survey and Analysis." Westport, CT: May 1985.

Hunter, Beverly. "Computer Literacy." Paper presented at the Patterns Conference on Computer Literacy, Rochester, New York, 27–28 April 1981.

Judd, Wallace. "A Teacher's Place in the Computer Curriculum." *Phi Delta Kappan*, October 1983.

Kozol, Jonathan. *Illiterate America*. Garden City, NY: Anchor Press/Doubleday, 1985.

Kuhn, Thomas S. *The Structure of Scientific Revolutions*. Chicago: University of Chicago Press, 1962.

Lave, Jean. "A Comparative Approach to Educational Forms and Learning Processes." *Anthropology and Education Quarterly*, v. 13, no. 2, 1982.

Lepper, Mark R., and David Greene. "Turning Play into Work: Effects of Adult Surveillance and Extrinsic Rewards on Children's Intrinsic Motivation." *Journal of Personality and Social Psychology*, v. 31, no. 3, 1975.

Lepper, Mark R., David Greene, and Richard E. Nisbett. "Undermining Children's Intrinsic Interest With Extrinsic Reward: A Test of the 'Overjustification Hypothesis'." *Journal of Personality and Social Psychology*, v. 28, no. 1, 1973.

Malone, Thomas. *What Makes Things Fun To Learn? A Study of Intrinsically Motivating Computer Games*. Ph.D. dissertation, Dept. of Psychology, Stanford University, June 1980.

Mayo, Elton. Quoted in "A Distinctive Competence." *Harvard Business School Bulletin*. Boston: Harvard Business School, April 1982.

McCorduck, Pamela. *Machines Who Think: A Personal Inquiry into the History and Prospects of Artificial Intelligence*. San Francisco: W. H. Freeman and Company, 1979.

National Commission on Excellence in Education. *A Nation at Risk: The Imperative for Educational Reform.* Washington, D.C.: U.S. Department of Education, v. 65, April 1983.

Neibauer, Alan. "The Computer Literacy Myth." *T.H.E. Journal,* February 1985.

New York State Department of Education. "The Incredible Computer." In *Inside Education,* Albany, N.Y.: New York State Department of Education, v. 67, no. 4, January–February 1981. (Reprinted in "Microcomputers in Today's Schools: An Administrators' Handbook," by the Northwest Regional Educational Laboratory, November 1981.)

Olds, Henry F., Jr. "Evaluating the Evaluation Schemes." *Evaluation of Educational Software,* 1983.

———. "Through a New Looking Glass." *Microcomputing,* September 1981.

———. "Sometimes Children Are the Best Teachers." *Popular Computing,* October 1984.

———. "The Microcomputer and the Hidden Curriculum." *Computers in the Schools,* v. 2, no. 1, September 1985.

Papert, Seymour, *Mindstorms: Children, Computers, and Powerful Ideas.* New York: Basic Books, Inc., 1980.

———. Quoted by Nina McCain in "Project Plans 'School of the Future,'" *Boston Globe,* 23 March 1985.

Perkins, David. "Educational Heaven: Promises and Perils of Instruction by Video Games." In *Video Games and Human Development: A Research Agenda for the '80s.* Cambridge: Monroe C. Gutman Library, Harvard Graduate School of Education, 1983.

Peters, Thomas J., and Robert H. Waterman, Jr. *In Search of Excellence: Lessons from America's Best-Run Companies.* New York: Warner Books, 1984.

Regena, C. "Programming the TI: Writing an Educational Program." *COMPUTE!,* September 1984.

Research Briefing on Information Technology in Precollege Education. Committee on Science, Engineering, and Public Policy of the National Academy of Sciences et al., September 1984.

Richie, Oscar W., and Marvin R. Koller. *Sociology of Childhood.* New York: Appleton-Century-Crofts, 1964.

Roberts, John M., Malcolm J. Arth, and Robert R. Bush. "Games in Culture." *American Anthropologist,* v. 61, 1959.

Roberts, John M., and Brian Sutton-Smith. "Child Training and Game Involvement." In *The Study of Games.* New York: John Wiley and Sons, 1978.

Schwartzman, Helen B. *Transformations.* New York: Plenum Press, 1978.

Senese, Donald J. "Technology: Developing Our Newest and Greatest Resource." *T.H.E. Journal,* September 1984.

Simpson, Brian. "Heading for the Ha-Ha." *Teachers College Record.* NY: Columbia University, v. 85, no. 4, Summer 1984.

Sluckin, Andy. *Growing Up in the Playground.* Boston: Routledge & Kegan Paul, Ltd., 1981.

Snyder, Tom, and David Dockterman. "Getting to 'Aha!'" *Electronic Learning,* May–June 1984.

Steffin, Sherwin. Quoted by Vincent Puglia in "Do Educational Games Really Teach?" *Electronic Games,* July 1984.

Steinbrunner, John D. *The Cybernetic Theory of Decision: New Dimensions of Political Analysis.* Princeton: Princeton University Press, 1974.

Sternhell, Carol. "Bellow's Typewriters and Other Tics of the Trade." *The New York Times Book Review.* 2 September 1984.

Strickland, L. H. "Surveillance and Trust." *Journal of Personality,* v. 26, 1958, cited by Lepper and Greene, 1975.

Suhor, Charles. "Cars, Computers, and Curriculum." *Educational Leadership,* September 1983.

Suppes, Patrick. "The Uses of Computers in Education." *Scientific American,* v. 215, no. 3, September 1966.

Thornburg, David D. "Discovery-based Learning and Teen-agers." *COMPUTE!*, September 1984.

Turkle, Sherry, *The Second Self: Computers and the Human Spirit.* New York: Simon and Schuster, 1984.

Weizenbaum, Joseph. *Computer Power and Human Reason: From Judgement to Calculation.* San Francisco: W. H. Freeman and Company, 1976.

Whitehead, Alfred N. *The Aims of Education.* London: Ernest Benn, 1950.

Williams, Dennis A., with Dianne H. McDonald, Lucy Howard, Michael Reese, and George Raine. "Access Without Success." *Newsweek*, 19 March 1984.

INDEX

Academic Therapy, 48
Advertising claims, 56–59
Agent USA, 133, 134, 138, 140
Alexander the Great, 76
Analytical engine, 34–35
Aristotle, 76
Arth, Malcolm, 110
Artificial intelligence, 18
Art of Fiction, The (Gardner), 119–120
Assembly language, 97

Babbage, Charles, 34
Bannercatch, 135
Barzun, Jacques, 44, 54, 139
Baseball, 138–139
BASIC, 35, 67, 92
Bok, Derek, 49, 65, 79
Boston Public Schools, 9, 33
Brainworks, 107
Brooks, Frederick, 93, 126
Bruner, Jerome, 70, 117

Bugs, 93
Bush, Robert, 110

CAI. *See* Computer-aided instruction
C language, 35, 97
Classroom Computer Learning, 4
Clements, Douglas H., 95
"Combinatorial explosion," 78
COMPUTE! 41, 77
Computer(s):
    expectations concerning, 7–21
    fallacies on school use of, 31–32, 34–35
    individual adjustment to, 19–20
    as instructional medium, 37–38, 75–89
    limitations of, as educational tool, 59–61
    as modeling device, 39–40, 105–143

Computer(s) *(continued)*
  number of, 26, 29, 30, 33
  problems in use of, 7–21, 40–
    41
  purposes of, 37–40
  purchase of, 24–25
  social interactions and, 61–63,
    111–115, 134–136
  student use of, 40–43
  teachers and, 28
  as tool, 38–39, 91–103
Computer-aided instruction
    (CAI), 3, 34, 37–38, 75–89
  advantages of, 87–89
  design of, 79–81
  factual content of, 81–83
  isolating nature of, 84–87
  publishers of, 80
  step-by-step approach of, 83–
    84
  teachers as programmers for,
    78
Computer Assisted Defense sys-
    tem (CAD) 136
Computer literacy, 1–2, 40, 52,
    98
Control Data, 8
Cowan, P. A., 111
Culture, 53–54
Curriculum packages, 45–49
Cybernetic Theory of Decision, The
    (Steinbrunner), 126

Doubleday, Abner, 139
Drill-and-practice programs, 37,
    42, 45
  See also Computer-aided in-
    struction

Electronic Learning, 95
Energy Search, 124
Environment, of schools, 63–65
Experiments, 8–11

Focus group, 16

Games, 39, 106–143
  defined, 109, 115

design and development of,
    124–132
  educational purposes of, 110,
    116–117
  evaluation of, 132–134
  interaction and, 134–136
  as learning tool, 107–108, 109,
    118–120
  simulations and, 106, 121–122
  teachers and, 141–143
  types of, 110
"Games in Culture" (Roberts,
    Arth, and Bush), 110.
Gardner, John, 119–120
Geoboards, 56
Geography Search, 134–135,
    138, 140
Gordon, Horace, 48
Greene, David, 68

Hardware, 15
  fallacies about, 31–32
  school purchase and use of,
    30–33
Harvard Graduate School of Ed-
    ucation, 8
Hawthorne effect, 114
Hennigan Elementary School, 9
Herndon, James, 65
Hollos, M., 111
Holt, John, 9, 102
Hood, John F., 30
*How to Survive in Your Native
    Land* (Herndon), 65
Hunter, Beverly, 97–98

Illiterate America (Kozol), 52
In Search of Excellence (Peters and
    Waterman), 114
Interaction, 61–63, 111–115,
    134–136
Intervention, 96

*Journal of Personality and Social
    Psychology*, 68
Johns Hopkins Survey, 28, 30,
    40, 42

Kozol, Jonathan, 52
Kuhn, Thomas, 82

Lap learning, 61–63
Learning:
  environment and, 63–65
  motivation and, 65–67
  surveillance and, 68–70
Learning games. *See* Games
Lego blocks, 95, 96
Lepper, Mark, 68
Literacy, 2–3, 51–53
  See also Computer literacy
LOGO, 10, 18, 41, 71, 92, 94–96
Lotus 1-2-3, 128

Matching Familiar Figures Test,
  95
Mathematics, 9
  fallacies limiting computer use
  to, 31, 34–35
Mathland, 9
Mayo, Elton, 114
Milone, Michael, 48
*Mindstorms: Children, Computers,
  and Powerful Ideas* (Papert), 9
Minority students, use of com-
  puters by, 42
MIT, 52
Modeling. *See* Simulation
Motivation, 65–67
Muppet Learning Keys, 63
Murrow, Edward R., 12
Mythical Man-Month, The
  (Brooks), 93

National Academy of Sciences,
  66
National Commission on Excel-
  lence in Education, 2, 51–52,
  53–54
*Nation at Risk: The Imperative for
  Educational Reform*, 2, 51–52,
  53–54
Negotiation, 54
Neibauer, Alan, 29
Networks, fallacies on school use
  of, 32

New York State Department of
  Education Commission, 14
Nisbett, Richard, 68

Olds, Henry F., Jr., 4, 36, 37, 81,
  130
Other Side, 135–136, 137

Papert, Seymour, 9–10, 11, 12,
  43, 93–94
Pascal, Blaise, 34
Pascal language, 35
Perkins, David, 8, 95
Peters, Thomas J., 114
PLATO program, 8
Play, 111–112
  See also Games
Process of Education, The (Bruner),
  70
Programming, 94–98
  with LOGO, 94–96
  in secondary schools, 41, 42
  usefulness of, 96–98
Project Zero, 8, 95

Reading, 8
  See also Literacy
"Research Briefing on Informa-
  tion Technology in Precol-
  lege Education," 66
Roberts, David, 48
Roberts, John, 110, 115
Role-taking, 111–112, 115
Rules, 116
Run For The Money, 137–138,
  140

Sachs, Jonathan, 128
Scaffolding, 62–63
Schools:
  availability of computers in, 27
  environment of, 63–65
  fallacies on computer use, 31–
  32, 34–35
  number of computers in, 26,
  29, 30, 33
  software for (*see* Software)

Schools *(continued)*
    student use of computers in, 40–43
Schwartz, Judah, 15
Second Self: Computers and the Human Spirit (Turkle), 10
"Sesame Street," 112
Seuss, David, 8–9
Simulation, 39–40, 105–143
    design and development of, 124–132
    games and, 106, 121–122
    as learning tool, 107–108, 109, 122–124
    limitations of, 122
    teachers and, 141–143
Snyder, Tom, Productions (TSP), 124, 129, 132, 133
Social skills, 54–55, 115–116
Socio-economic groups, and computer use, 42–43
Software:
    availability of, 17–19, 46–47
    claims for, 56–59
    demand for, 29–30
    development of, 15–17, 124–132
    drill-and-practice, 37, 42, 45
    limitations of, 59–61
    publishers of, 46–47, 80
    purposes of, 37–40
    quality of, 27–28
    tutorials, 37–38
    wrap-around, 44–47
    See also Computer-aided instruction
"Sometimes Children Are the Best Teachers" (Olds), 130
SpellDiver, 133–134, 138
Spinnaker Software, 8
Spreadsheets, 38, 39, 99
Steffin, Sherwin, 107

Steinbrunner, Carol, 139
Steinbrunner, John, 126
Strickland, L. H., 69
Structure of Scientific Revolutions, The (Kuhn), 82
Suhor, Charles, 52–53, 62
Suppes, Patrick, 76
Surveillance, 68–70
Sutton-Smith, Brian, 115
Symphony, 128

Targeted Learning, 97
Teachers:
    computer as tool for, 70–73, 102–103
    learning games and, 141–143
    qualifications of, 54
    as source of educational software, 78
    training of, 28, 72–73
Television, 112
T.H.E. Journal, 29
Thornburg, David, 41
Tool, computer as, 38, 92, 94, 98, 99, 100, 101
Torrance Test, 95
Toward a Theory of Instruction (Bruner), 117
Turkle, Sherry, 10, 11, 36, 112, 124
Tutorials, 37–38
    See also Computer-aided instruction

VisiCalc, 99

Waterman, Robert, 114
Weizenbaum, Joseph, 13, 55
Whitehead, Alfred North, 53
Word processing, 38, 39, 99–100
Wrap-around software, 44–47